KOChie's Best JoKes 2

DAVID KOCH

Published by:

WP Wilkinson Publishing Pty Ltd
ACN 006 042 173
Level 4, 2 Collins Street
Melbourne, Vic 3000

Tel: 03 9654 5446

www.wilkinsonpublishing.com.au

National Library of Australia Cataloguing-in-Publication data:

Koch, David.

Kochie's best jokes 2.

ISBN 9781921332067 (pbk.).

1. Australian wit and humor. I. Title.

808.882

Cover design: QGraphics

Design & layout: Chris Georgiou

Printed in Australia: Trojan Press, Preston VIC

David Koch

David Koch is well-known to millions of Australians as co-host of Australia's No. 1 breakfast show *Sunrise* on the Seven Network and is one of the most recognised people on Australian television – a recent survey by *Readers Digest* found he is one of the 25 most trusted Australians.

His list of achievements illustrates the breadth of his expertise, from being a small business owner; finance editor, Silver Logie nominee four years running; and best selling author. David's knowledge of money and business is extensive and has been recognised on a number of occasions including most recently in June 2007 where David was voted best finance journalist by the readers of *Australian Banking & Finance* magazine.

Renowned for his love of a joke, Kochie's humour and charm are also at home on Seven's high rating television program *Where Are They Now.*

Kochie has been married to Libby for 30 years and they have four children – Samantha (married to Toby), Brianna, Alexander and Georgina.

For more information on Kochie please go to *www.kochie.com.au*

Wayne Harrison

Three years ago, Wayne Harrison of Advanced Airbrush was invited by David Koch to spend a morning on *Sunrise*, drawing cartoons of Mel and Kochie. Kochie enjoyed it so much, he kept the caricature of himself – the very one which is on the cover of this book and *Kochie's Best Jokes*. Wayne's clever cartoons have now been used in both of Kochie's joke books, *Kochie's Best Jokes* and *Kochie's Best Jokes 2*.

Wayne Harrison has been airbrushing for more than 25 years, and his artworks have won awards in Australia and the USA. His artwork has also received a lot of major awards for Top Graphics and Airbrush Art (Murals) at various automotive shows, and he was placed in the top five airbrush artists in the world.

Wayne's cartoons appear on the cover and pages 12, 16, 22, 37, 41, 63, 72, 77, 94, 100, 116, 123, 199 and 244.

Introduction

"Joke of the Day" has become an institution on the *Sunrise* breakfast program. At around 6.45 am every day we try and have a good laugh.

One of the wonderful parts of the Australian character is our sense of humour. Our ability to laugh and often to laugh at ourselves. I love doing Joke of the Day for that very reason . . . it is just so Australian.

It's all good fun and should NEVER be taken seriously . . . although sometimes the jokes do get me into trouble when someone doesn't quite get the funny side. But that's the risk I run and I think it's worth it.

Thankyou to everyone who supported my first book of jokes and I'm really excited about this second edition.

Here you will find a joke for every day of the year and then some. In fact you will find twelve extra days – wouldn't it be great if we could squeeze some more days into our already hectic year.

We all need a regular laugh to counter all the bad news presented to us every day on the TV, radio and in newspapers. Take the time to catch Joke of the Day on the *Sunrise* program every weekday morning and then top up with a joke or two from this book.

Remember, when you laugh, the whole world laughs with you and wouldn't it be a better place if we all did just that.

Enjoy!

David Koch

1.

Ed was in trouble. He forgot his wedding anniversary. His wife was really angry.

She told him; 'Tomorrow morning, I expect to find a gift in the driveway that goes from 0 to 200 in less than six seconds **AND IT BETTER BE THERE!!'**

The next morning Ed got up early and left for work. When his wife woke up she looked out the window and sure enough there was a boxed gift in the middle of the driveway.

Confused, the wife put on her robe and ran out to the driveway, brought the box back in the house. She opened it and found a brand new bathroom scale.

Ed has been missing since Friday. Stupid, stupid man!

2.

Here are a series of promises that speak of our friendship. You will see no cutesy smiley faces – just the stone cold truth of true friendship.

When you are sad – I will help you get drunk and plot revenge against the sorry bastard who made you that way.

When you are blue – I will try to dislodge whatever is choking you.

When you smile – I will know you finally got laid.

When you are scared – I will rag on you about it every chance I get.

When you are worried – I will tell you horrible stories about how much worse it could be until you quit whining.

When you are confused – I will use small words in simple sentences.

When you are sick – Stay the hell away from me until you are well again. I don't want to catch whatever you have.

When you fall – I will point and laugh at your clumsy ass.

And remember . . . when life hands you lemons, get some tequila and salt and call me!

3.
Why did the blonde resolve to have only three children?

She heard that one out of every four children born in the world is Chinese.

4.
An army Major visiting sick soldiers, goes up to one private and asks –

'What's your problem, soldier?'

'Chronic syphilis, Sir.'

'What treatment are you getting?'

'Five minutes with the wire brush each day.'

'What's your ambition?'

'To get back to the front, Sir.'

'Good man,' says the Major. He goes to the next bed.

'What's your problem, soldier?'

'Chronic piles, Sir.'

'What treatment are you getting?'

'Five minutes with the wire brush each day.'

'What's your ambition?'

'To get back to the front, Sir.'

'Good man,' says the Major. He goes to the next bed. 'What's your problem, soldier?'

'Chronic gum disease, Sir.'

'What treatment are you getting?'

'Five minutes with the wire brush each day.'

'What's your ambition?'

'To get the wire brush before the other two, Sir.'

5.
 Did you hear about the two blondes who froze to death in a drive-in movie?

They went to see *Closed for the Winter*.

6.
 A young man wanted to get his beautiful blonde wife, Susie, something nice for their first wedding anniversary. So he decided to buy her a mobile phone. He showed her the phone and explained to her all of its features.

Susie was excited to receive the gift and simply adored her new phone.

The next day Susie went shopping. Her phone rang and, to her astonishment, it was her husband on the other end. 'Hi Susie,' he said, 'how do you like your new phone?'

Susie replied, 'I just love it! It's so small and your voice is clear as a bell, but there's one thing I don't understand though . . . '

'What's that, sweetie?' asked her husband.

'How did you know I was at K-Mart!'

7.

A foreign company and an American company decided to have a canoe race on the Missouri River. Both teams practised long and hard to reach their peak performance before the race.

On the big day, the foreign company won by a mile.

The Americans, very discouraged and distressed, decided to investigate the reason for the crushing defeat. A team made up of senior managers was formed to investigate and recommend appropriate corrective action.

Their conclusion was that the foreign company had eight people rowing and one person steering, while the American team had eight people steering and one person rowing.

Feeling a deeper study was in order the American management hired a consulting company and paid them a large amount of money for a second opinion. They advised, of course, that too many people were steering the boat, while not enough people were rowing!

Not sure of how to utilise that information, but wanting to

prevent another loss to any foreign company, the rowing team's management structure was totally reorganised . . . to four steering supervisors, three area steering superintendents and one assistant superintendent steering manager . . .

They also implemented a new performance system that would give the one person rowing the boat greater incentive to work harder. It was called the 'Rowing Person Quality First Program', with meetings, dinners and a free pen for the rower. There was discussion of getting a new paddle, canoe and other equipment, with extra vacation days for practices . . . and bonuses!

The next year the foreign company won by two miles!

Humiliated, the American management laid off the rower for poor performance, halted development of a new canoe, sold the paddle, and cancelled all capital investments for new equipment. The money saved was distributed to the Senior Executives as bonuses and the following year's racing team was out-sourced to India.

8.
On their way to get married, a young Catholic couple is involved in a fatal car accident. The couple found themselves sitting outside the Pearly Gates waiting for St Peter to process them into Heaven. While waiting, they begin to wonder; could they possibly get married in Heaven?

When St Peter showed up, they asked him. St Peter says, 'I don't know. This is the first time anyone has asked. Let me go find out,' and he leaves.

The couple sat and waited, and waited. Two months passed; the couple was still waiting. As they waited, they discussed that IF they were allowed to get married in Heaven, what was the eternal aspect of it all. 'What if it doesn't work?' they wondered, 'Are we stuck together FOREVER?'

After yet another month, St Peter finally returns, looking somewhat bedraggled. 'Yes,' he informs the couple, 'you CAN get married in Heaven.'

'Great!' said the couple, 'But we were just wondering, what if things don't work? Could we also get a divorce in Heaven?'

St Peter, red-faced with anger, slams his clipboard onto the ground.

'What's wrong?' asked the frightened couple.

'OH, COME ON!' St Peter shouts, 'It took me three months to find a priest up here!

'Do you have ANY idea how long it's going to take me to find a LAWYER?'

9. The husband had just finished reading a book entitled *You can be the man of your house*. He stormed out to his wife in the kitchen and announced, 'From now on, you need to know that I am the man of this house and my word is law.'

'You will prepare me a gourmet meal tonight and when I'm finished eating my meal, you will serve me a sumptuous dessert.

After dinner you are going to go upstairs with me and we will have the kind of sex I want.

'Afterwards, you are going to draw me a bath so I can relax. You will wash my back and towel me dry and bring me my robe.

Then, you will massage my feet and hands and fluff my pillows and make me comfortable for a good night's sleep.

'Then tomorrow, guess who's going to dress me and comb my hair?'

The wife replied, 'The f@#$ing funeral director would be my first guess.'

10. A man suffered a serious heart attack and had open heart bypass surgery.

He awakened from the surgery to find himself in the care of nuns at a Catholic hospital.

As he was recovering, a nun asked him questions regarding how he was going to pay for his treatment. She asked if he had health insurance.

He replied, in a raspy voice, 'No health insurance.'

The nun asked if he had money in the bank.

He replied, 'No money in the bank.'

The nun asked, 'Do you have a relative who could help you?'

He said, 'I only have a spinster sister, who is a nun.'

The nun became agitated and announced loudly, 'Nuns are not spinsters. Nuns are married to God!'

The patient replied, 'Then send the bill to my brother-in-law.'

11.

A blonde walks into a library and orders a hamburger, fries and a coke.

The librarian replies; 'Can't you read the sign? We are a library.'

The blonde whispers . . . 'A hamburger, fries and a coke.'

12.

A grandson asks his grandmother how old she is.

The grandmother refuses to tell him, reminding him you're never supposed to ask a woman her age.

A few weeks later the grandson visits his grandmother again.

He says; 'I know how old you are!'

She asks; 'How did you find out?'

He says; 'I looked at your licence. Now I know you're 84 AND you got an F for sex.'

13.

Two brooms were hanging in the closet and after a while they got to know each other so well they decided to get married.

One broom was, of course, the bride broom, the other the groom broom.

The bride broom looked very beautiful in her white dress. The groom broom was handsome and suave in his tuxedo. The wedding was lovely.

After the wedding, at the wedding dinner, the bride broom leaned over and said to the groom broom, 'I think I am going to have a little dust broom!!!'

'IMPOSSIBLE!!' said the groom broom. 'We haven't even SWEPT together yet!'

14.

There was a ragged, old, retired Chief Stoker who shuffled into a waterfront bar. Stinking of whisky and cigarettes, his hands shook as he took the 'Piano Player Wanted' sign from the window and handed it to the bartender.

'I'd like to apply for the job,' he said.

The bartender wasn't too sure about this doubtful looking old Salt, but it had been quite a while since he had a piano player and business was falling off.

So, the bartender decided to give him a try. The old Chief staggered his way over to the piano while several patrons snickered.

By the time he was into his third bar of music, every voice was silenced.

What followed was a rhapsody of sound and music, unlike anyone had heard in the bar before. When he finished there wasn't a dry eye in the place.

The bartender took the old Chief a beer and asked him the name of the song he had just played.

'It's called *Drop Your Dacks, Baby, We're Gonna Rock Tonight*', said the old Chief after he took a long sip from the beer.

The bartender and the crowd winced, but the piano player went on with a knee-slapping, hand-clapping bit of ragtime that had the place jumping.

After he finished the Chief acknowledged the applause and told the crowd the song was called *Big Boobs Make My Anchor Chain Run Out.*

He then excused himself as he lurched to the head.

When he came out the bartender went over to him and said, 'Look Chief, the job is yours, but do you know your fly is open and your dick is hanging out?'

'Know it?' the old Chief replied, 'I wrote it!!!'

15.

     Two Irishmen were standing at the base of a flagpole, looking up. A blonde walks by and asks what they are doing.

Paddy; 'We're supposed to find the height of this flagpole, but we don't have a ladder.'

The blonde took a spanner from her purse, loosened a few bolts and laid the flagpole down.

She pulled a tape measure from her pocket, took a few measurements and announced that it was six metres. She then walked off.

Mick; 'Ain't that just like a blonde! We need the height and she gives us the length.'

16. The judge says to a double-homicide defendant, 'You're charged with beating your wife to death with a hammer.'

A voice at the back of the courtroom yells out, 'You bastard.'

The judge then said, 'You're also charged with beating your mother-in-law to death with a hammer.'

The voice in the back of the courtroom yells out, 'You bastard.'

The judge stops and says to the guy in the back of the courtroom, 'Sir, I can understand your anger and frustration at this crime. But no more outbursts from you or I'll charge you with contempt. Is that understood?'

The guy in the back of the court stands up and says, 'I'm sorry, Your Honour, but for 15 years, I've lived next door to that bastard and every time I asked to borrow a hammer, he said he didn't have one.'

17. A woman was in bed with her lover when she heard her husband opening the front door.

'Hurry,' she said, 'stand in the corner.'

She rubbed baby oil all over him, then dusted him with talcum powder.

'Don't move until I tell you,' she said. 'Pretend you're a statue.'

'What's this?' the husband inquired as he entered the room.

'Oh, it's a statue,' she replied. 'The Smiths bought one and I liked it so I got one for us, too.'

No more was said, not even when they went to bed. Around 2am the husband got up, went to the kitchen and returned with a sandwich and a beer.

'Here,' he said to the statue. 'Have this. I stood like that for two days at the Smiths and nobody offered me a damned thing.'

18.

Q: What do you call Bob the Builder when he retires?

A: Bob.

19.

An 18-year-old girl tells her mum that she has missed her period for two months. Very worried, the mother goes to the drugstore and buys a pregnancy kit. The test result shows that the girl is pregnant.

Shouting, cursing, crying, the mother says; 'Who was the pig that did this to you? I want to know!'

The girl picks up the phone and makes a call.

Half an hour later a Ferrari stops in front of their house, a mature and distinguished man with grey hair and impeccably dressed in an Armani suit steps out of the Ferrari and enters the house.

He sits in the living room with the father, mother and the girl, and tells them; 'Good morning, your daughter has informed me of the problem. I can't marry her because of my personal family situation but I'll take charge. I will pay all costs and provide for your daughter for the rest of her life. Additionally, if a girl is born I will bequeath her two retail stores, a townhouse, a beachfront villa and a $2 million bank account.

If a boy is born, my legacy will be a couple of factories and a $4 million bank account. If twins, they will receive a factory and $2 million each.

'However, if there is a miscarriage, what do you suggest I do?'

At this point, the father, who had remained silent, places a hand firmly on the man's shoulder and tells him . . .

'You root her again!'

20.

A man is waiting for his wife to give birth. The doctor comes in and informs the dad that his son was born without torso, arms or legs. The son is just a head!

But the dad loves his son and raises him as well as he can, with love and compassion. So picture this son as a teenager; the father comes home on the son's birthday and says; 'Hey, I've got a really great birthday present for you!'

The son says; 'Ah gee Dad not another hat!'

Now this is rather a raw deal for a kid with just a head and the loving father knew more than just a hat would be needed to make his kid right. After 18 years, the son is now old enough for his first beer.

Dad takes him to the bar, tearfully tells the son he is proud of him and orders the biggest, strongest tankard for his boy. With all the bar patrons looking on curiously and the bartender shaking his head in disbelief, the boy takes his first sip of beer.

Swoooosh! Plop!!

A torso pops out!

The bar is dead silent, then bursts into whoops of joy.

The father, shocked, begs his son to drink again.

The patrons chant, 'Take another drink!'

The bartender continues to shake his head in dismay.

Swoooosh! Plip! Plop!! Two arms pop out.

The bar goes wild. The father, crying, begs his son to drink again.

The patrons chant, 'Take another drink! Take another drink!!'

The bartender ignores the whole affair and goes back to polishing glasses, shaking his head, clearly unimpressed by the amazing scenes. By now the boy is getting tipsy, but with his new hands he reaches down, grabs his drink and guzzles the last of it.

Plop! Plip!! Two legs pop out.

The bar is in chaos. The father falls to his knees and tearfully thanks God.

The boy stands up on his new legs and stumbles to the left then staggers to the right through the front door, into the street, where a truck runs over him and kills him instantly – the bar falls silent.

The father moans in grief.

The bartender sighs and says, 'He should've quit while he was still a head!'

21.
RanDom thouGhts of a wanDerinG minD . . .

★ Save the whales. Collect the whole set.

★ A day without sunshine is like . . . Night.

★ On the other hand . . . you have different fingers.

★ 42.7 per cent of all statistics are made up on the spot.

★ 99 per cent of lawyers give the rest a bad name.

★ Remember, half the people you know are below average.

★ He who laughs last, thinks slowest.

★ Depression is merely anger without enthusiasm.

★ The early bird may get the worm, but the second mouse gets the cheese in the trap.

★ Support bacteria. They're the only culture some people have.

★ A clear conscience is usually the sign of a bad memory.

★ Change is inevitable . . . except from vending machines.

★ If you think nobody cares . . . try missing a couple of payments.

★ How many of you believe in psycho-kinesis? Raise my hand.

★ OK, so what's the speed of dark?

★ When everything is coming your way, you're in the wrong lane.

★ Hard work pays off in the future. Laziness pays off now.

★ Every one has a photographic memory. Some just don't have film.

* How much deeper would the ocean be without sponges?

* Eagles may soar but weasels don't get sucked into jet engines.

* What happens if you get scared half to death . . . twice?

* I couldn't repair your brakes, so I made your horn louder.

* Why do psychics have to ask you for your name?

* Inside every older person is a younger person wondering, 'What the hell happened?'

* Just remember . . . if the world didn't suck, we would all fall off.

* Light travels faster than sound. That's why some people appear bright until you hear them speak.

* Life isn't like a box of chocolates . . . It's more like a jar of jalapenos. What you do today, might burn your bum tomorrow.

22.

Jim and Edna were both patients in a mental hospital. One day while they were walking past the hospital swimming pool, Jim suddenly jumped into the deep end. He sank to the bottom of the pool and stayed there. Edna promptly jumped in to save him . . . she swam to the bottom and pulled Jim out.

When the Head Nurse became aware of Edna's heroic act she immediately ordered her to be discharged from the hospital as she now considered her to be mentally stable.

When she went to tell Edna the news she said, 'Edna, I have good news and bad news. The good news is you're being discharged since you were able to rationally respond to a crisis by jumping in and saving the life of another patient so I have concluded that your act displays sound mindedness.

'The bad news is that Jim, the patient you saved, hung himself in the bathroom with his dressing gown belt right after you saved him. I am so sorry, but he's dead.'

Edna replied, 'Oh he didn't hang himself, I put him there to dry. How soon can I go home?'

23.

Two cows are standing in a field.

One says to the other, 'Are you worried about Mad Cow Disease?'

The other one says, 'No, it doesn't worry me, I'm a helicopter!'

24.

FOr those who love the Philosophy of amBiGuity

* Don't sweat the petty things and don't pet the sweaty things.

* One tequila, two tequila, three tequila, floor.

* Atheism is a non-prophet organisation.

* If man evolved from monkeys and apes, why do we still have monkeys and apes?

* The main reason Santa is so jolly is because he knows where all the bad girls live.

* I went to a bookstore and asked the saleswoman, 'Where's the self-help section?' She said if she told me, it would defeat the purpose.

* What if there were no hypothetical questions?

* If a deaf person swears, does his mother wash his hands with soap?

* If someone with multiple personalities threatens to kill himself, is it considered a hostage situation?

* Is there another word for synonym?

* If a parsley farmer is sued, can they garnish his wages?

* Wouldn't a fly without wings be called a walk?

* Why do they lock petrol station bathrooms? Are they afraid someone will clean them?

* If a turtle doesn't have a shell, is he homeless or naked?

* Can vegetarians eat animal crackers?

* If the police arrest a mime, do they tell him he has the right to remain silent?

* Why do they put braille on the drive-through bank machines?

* How do they get wombats to cross the road only at those yellow road signs?

* What was the best thing before sliced bread?

* One nice thing about egotists; they don't talk about other people.

* Does the little mermaid wear an algebra?

* Do infants enjoy infancy as much as adults enjoy adultery?

* How is it possible to have a civil war?

* If one synchronised swimmer drowns, do the rest drown too?

* If you ate both pasta and antipasto, would you still be hungry?

* If you try to fail, and succeed, which have you achieved?

* Whose cruel idea was it for the word 'lisp' to have 's' in it?

* Why are haemorrhoids called 'haemorrhoids' instead of 'assteroids'?

* Why is it called tourist season if we can't shoot at them?

* Why is there an expiration date on sour cream?

* If you spin an oriental man in a circle three times does he become disoriented?

* Can an atheist get insurance against acts of God?

25.

Bill and Tom are two Kiwis working at the local sawmill.

One day Bill slips and his arm gets caught and severed by the big bench saw. Tom quickly puts the limb in a plastic bag and rushes it, and Bill, to the local hospital.

Next day, Tom goes to the hospital and asks after Bill.

The nurse says, 'Oh he's out in Rehab exercising.'

Tom couldn't believe it, but here's Bill out the back exercising his now re-attached arm. The very next day he's back at work in the sawmill.

A couple of days go by, and then Bill slips and severs his leg on another bloody big saw thing. So Tom puts the limb in a plastic bag and rushes it, and Bil,l off to hospital.

The next day he calls in to see him and asks the nurse how he is.

The nurse replies, 'He's out in the Rehab again exercising.'

And, sure enough, here's Bill out there doing some serious work on the treadmill. And Bill comes back to work.

But, as usual, within a couple of days he has another accident and severs his head. Wearily Tom puts the head in a plastic bag and transports it, and Bill, to hospital.

Next day he goes in and asks the nurse how Bill is.

The nurse breaks down and cries and says, 'He's dead!'

Tom is shocked, but not surprised. 'I suppose the saw finally did him in.'

'No,' says the nurse. 'Some dopey bastard put his head in a plastic bag and he suffocated!'

AUSTRALIA DAY

Two Aussies, Davo and Jonno, were adrift in a lifeboat. While rummaging through the boat's provisions, Davo stumbled across an old lamp. He rubbed the lamp vigorously and a Genie came forth.

This Genie, however, stated that he could only deliver one wish, not the standard three.

Without giving much thought to the matter, Davo blurted out; 'Turn the entire ocean into beer. Make that Victoria Bitter!'

The Genie clapped his hands with a deafening crash, and immediately the sea turned into the hard-earned thirst quencher. The Genie then vanished.

Only the gentle lapping of beer on the hull broke the stillness as the two men considered their circumstances.

Jonno looked disgustedly at Davo whose wish had been granted.

After a long, tension-filled moment Jonno said; 'Nice going, idiot! Now we're going to have to piss in the boat.'

27.

Passengers aboard a luxurious cruise ship were having a great time when a beautiful young woman fell overboard. Immediately there was an 80-year-old man in the water who rescued her.

The crew pulled them both out of the treacherous waters. The captain was grateful as well as astonished that the white-haired old man performed such an act of bravery.

That night a banquet was given in honor of the ship's elderly hero. He was called forward to receive an award and was asked to say a few words.

He said, 'First of all, I'd like to know who the bastard who pushed me is!'

28.

I took a look at my wife one day and said; 'Honey, 36 years ago we had a cheap apartment, no car, no TV, no money and slept on a sofa bed, but I got to sleep every night with a hot good looking 18-year-old. Now, we have a beautiful house, two nice cars, king size bed, money and a wall screen TV, but I'm sleeping with a 54-year-old woman. It seems to me that you are not holding up your side of things.'

My wife is a very reasonable woman.

She told me to go out and find a hot 18-year-old beautiful girl. Then she would make sure that I would once again be living in a cheap apartment, with no car, no money, and sleeping on a sofa bed.

Aren't women great? They really know how to solve your mid-life crisis!

29.

Q: How many men does it take to screw in a light bulb?

A: One. He just holds it up there and waits for the world to revolve around him.

Or three. One to screw in the bulb and two to listen to him brag about the screwing part.

30.

A woman named Jill stood up at her church's Testimony Meeting, or as some churches call it, Cry Sunday.

This particular Sunday morning, she took the microphone from one of the church ushers, and bared her soul to the enrapt congregation.

'I want to tell you about the awful accident that my husband, Jim, has suffered this past month. He was riding his bike, lost control, ran off the highway and hit a tree. He was rushed to the hospital, and could have died, but thank the Lord, all he suffered was a broken scrotum.'

The congregation gasped in horror. The men in the congregation were obviously uneasy and writhed in their seats.

'Jim has been in terrible pain all month since the accident. He has trouble breathing. He has trouble swallowing his food. He can hardly lift anything, he's in so much pain, and he has missed work because of it. He can't lift our children up to hold them and give them the personal love that they need. Worst of all, we can no longer cuddle and have intimate relations. He is in constant pain, a pain so terrible that our love life has all but slipped away into oblivion.

'I would like to ask you all in the congregation to pray for Jim, and pray for us, that his broken scrotum will soon heal and be as good as new.'

A dull murmur erupted within the congregation as the full impact of this terrible accident sunk in, and the men in the congregation were visibly shaken up with the thought, 'There but for the grace of God, go I.'

Then, as the murmuring settled down, a lone figure stood up in midst of the congregation, worked his way up to the pulpit, obviously in pain, adjusted the microphone to his liking, then leaned over and said to the congregation;

'My name is Jim, and I have only one word for my wife Jill. That word is; STERNUM . . . !!!'

31.

Q: Why do little boys whine?

A: Because they are practising to be men.

32.

Murphy showed up at Mass one Sunday and the priest almost fell down when he saw him. Murphy had never been seen in church in all his life.

After Mass, the priest caught up with Murphy and said; 'Murphy, I am so glad ya decided to come to Mass, what made ya come?'

Murphy said; 'I got to be honest with you Father, a while back, I misplaced me hat and I really, really love that hat. I know that McGlynn had a hat just like me hat, and I knew that McGlynn came to church every Sunday. I also knew that McGlynn had to take off his hat during Mass and figured he would leave it in the back of the church. So, I was going to leave after Communion and steal McGlynn's hat.'

The priest said, 'Well, Murphy, I notice that ya didn't steal McGlynn's hat. What changed your mind?'

Murphy said, 'Well, after I heard your sermon on the 10 Commandments, I decided that I didn't need to steal McGlynn's hat after all.'

The priest gave Murphy a big smile and said; 'After I talked about Thou Shalt Not Steal ya decided you would rather do without your hat than burn in Hell, right?'

Murphy slowly shook his head and said, 'No, Father, after ya talked about Thou Shalt Not Commit Adultery I remembered where I left me hat.'

33.

A little boy walks into his parents' room to see his mum on top of his dad bouncing up and down. The mum sees her son and quickly dismounts, worried about what her son has seen. She dresses quickly and goes to find him.

The son sees his mum and asks; 'What were you and Dad doing?'

The mother replies; 'Well, you know your dad has a big tummy and sometimes I have to get on top of it and help flatten it.'

'You're wasting your time,' said the boy.

'Why is that?' the mum asked, puzzled.

'Well when you go shopping the lady next door comes over and gets on her knees and blows it right back up.'

34.
A mechanic was removing a cylinder-head from the motor of a Harley motorcycle when he spotted a well-known cardiologist in his shop.

The cardiologist was there waiting for the service manager to come take a look at his bike when the mechanic shouted across the garage; 'Hey Doc, want to take a look at this?'

The cardiologist, a bit surprised, walked over to where the mechanic was working on the motorcycle.

The mechanic straightened up, wiped his hands on a rag and asked; 'So Doc, look at this engine. I open its heart, take the valves out, repair any damage, and then put them back in, and when I finish, it works just like new. So how come I make $39,675 a year and you get a million when you and I are doing basically the same work?'

The cardiologist paused, smiled and leaned over, then whispered to the mechanic; 'Try doing it with the engine running.'

35.
Q: What do you call a handcuffed man?

A: Trustworthy.

36.
A blind bloke walks into a shop with a guide dog.

He picks the dog up and starts swinging it around his head.

Alarmed, a shop assistant calls out: 'Can I help, sir?'

'No thanks,' says the blind bloke. 'Just looking.'

37.

Q: Why does it take 100 million sperms to fertilise one egg?

A: Because not one will stop and ask directions.

38.

Q: Why do female black widow spiders kill their mates after mating?

A: To stop the snoring before it starts.

39.

An Englishman, a Scotsman, and an Irishman are wandering through the desert, hungry and hallucinating, when they come upon a rotting, dead camel.

'Well' said the Englishman,' I support the Liverpool Football Club, so I'll eat the liver.'

'I support the Hearts Club,' said the Scotsman, 'so I'll eat the heart.'

'I support Arsenal' said the Irishman, 'but I seem to have lost my appetite.'

40.

Q: Why do men whistle when they are sitting on the toilet?

A: Because it helps them remember which end they need to wipe.

₄₁.

Sex and the country

A Frenchman and an Italian were seated next to an Englishman on an overseas flight. After a few cocktails, the men began discussing their home lives.

'Last night I made love to my wife four times,' the Frenchman bragged, 'and this morning she made me delicious crepes and she told me how much she adored me.'

'Ah, last night I made love to my wife six times,' the Italian responded, 'and this morning she made me a wonderful omelette and told me she could never love another man.'

When the Englishman remained silent, the Frenchman smugly asked, 'And how many times did you make love to your wife last night?'

'Once,' he replied.

'Only once?' the Italian arrogantly snorted.

'And what did she say to you this morning?

'Don't stop.'

₄₂.

Q: What is the difference between men and women?

A: A woman wants one man to satisfy her every need.

A man wants every woman to satisfy his one need.

43.

Q: How does a man keep his youth?

A: By giving her money, furs and diamonds.

44.

The Businessman's medical Problem

A businessman returns from the Far East. After a few days he notices strange growth on his penis. He sees several doctors. They all say, 'You've been screwing around in the Far East, very common there, no cure. We'll have to cut it off.'

The man panics, but figures if it is common in the East they must know how to cure it. So he goes back and sees a doctor in Pakistan.

The doctor examines him and says, 'You've been fooling around in my country. This is a very common problem here. Did you see any other doctors?'

The man replies, 'Yes a few in Australia.'

The doctor says, 'I bet they told you it had to be cut off.'

The man answers, 'Yes!'

The doctor smiles, nods, 'That is not correct. It will fall off by itself.'

45.

ST VALENTINE'S DAY

A St Valentine's Day plant arrived for me with a card signed, 'From your love.'

I assumed it was from my normally inattentive husband, but when I thanked him for it he denied having sent it. However, over the next few weeks his curiosity about the source grew into a new tenderness towards me.

I checked with the florist to make sure the plant hadn't been sent to me by mistake, but the mystery was solved a month later when my visiting mother-in-law asked; 'How's the plant?'

She explained; 'The last time I came here, you hinted that my son wasn't very attentive. I thought the plant might work. It did 20 years ago when my mother-in-law tried it.'

46.

Q: How do you keep your husband from reading your email?

A: Rename the folder to 'Instruction Manuals.'

47.

We were on our way to the hospital, where our 15-year-old daughter was to have a tonsillectomy.

'Dad,' our teenager said, 'How are they going to keep my mouth open during the surgery?'

'That's easy,' he replied.

'They're going to give you a phone.'

48.

While dancing at a party, I tripped and stubbed my toe. Days later, my toe was still swollen, so I saw a doctor. I told him how I had hurt myself and admitted to feeling foolish at being so clumsy.

After X-raying my toe, the doctor said he didn't need to do anything. Anxious to speed the healing, I asked if there was anything I could do.

'Should I soak it? Ice it? Is there anything you can recommend?'

He smiled and said, 'Take dancing lessons.'

49.

Two blondes living in Townsville were sitting on a bench talking.

One blonde says to the other; 'Which do you think is farther away . . . Melbourne or the moon?'

The other blonde turns and says; 'Hellooooooooooo, can you see Melbourne from here?'

50.

Three black ladies were preparing for their first plane flight. The first lady said; 'I don't know bout y'all, but I'm gonna wear me some hot pink panties on dis flight.'

'Why you gonna wear dat?' the other two asked.

The first replied; 'Cause, if dat plane goes down and I'm out dere laying butt-up in a corn field, dey gonna find me first.'

The second lady says; 'Well, I'm gonna wear me some fluorescent orange panties.'

'Why you gonna wear dem?' the others asked.

The second lady answered; 'Cause if dat plane goes down and I'm floatin butt-up in the ocean, dey can see me first.'

The third old lady says; 'Well, I'm not going to wear any panties at all.

'What, no panties?' the others said in disbelief.

'Dat's right,' says the third lady.

'I'm not wearing any panties, 'cause if dat plane goes down, the first thing they always looks for is da black box.'

51.
An eccentric philosophy professor gave a one-question final exam after a semester dealing with a broad array of topics.

The class was already seated and ready to go when the professor picked up his chair, plopped it on his desk and wrote on the board; 'Using everything we have learned this semester, prove that this chair does not exist.'

Fingers flew, erasers erased, notebooks were filled in furious fashion. Some students wrote over 30 pages in one hour attempting to refute the existence of the chair. One member of the class however, was up and finished in less than a minute.

Weeks later when the grades were posted, the student who finished in one minute got an A.

The rest of the group wondered how he could have gotten an A when he had barely written anything at all.

This is what he wrote; 'What chair?'

52.
Gennaro is in this country for only six months. He walks to work 20 blocks every day and passes a shoe store. Each day he stops and looks in the window to admire the Boccelli leather shoes. He wants those shoes so much, it's all he can think about.

After about two months he has saved enough to buy the shoes, $300, and purchases them.

Every Friday night the Italian community holds a dance in the church basement. Gennaro seizes this opportunity to wear his new Boccelli leather shoes for the first time.

He asks Sophia to dance and as they dance he asks her; 'Sophia, do you wear red panties tonight?'

Startled, Sophia replies; 'Yes Gennaro, I do wear red panties tonight but how do you know?'

Gennaro answers; 'I see the reflection in my new $300 Boccelli leather shoes. How do you like them?'

Next he asks Rosa to dance, and after a few minutes he asks; 'Rosa, do you wear white panties tonight?'

Rosa answers; 'Yes Gennaro, I do but how do you know that?'

He replies; 'I see the reflection in my new $300 Boccelli leather shoes. How do you like them?'

As the evening is almost over and the last song is being played, Gennaro asks Carmela to dance.

Midway through the dance his face turns red.

He states; 'Carmela, be stilla my heart. Please, please tell me you wear no panties tonight. Please, please, tella me this true!'

Carmela smiles coyly and answers; 'Yes Gennaro, I wear no panties tonight.'

Gennaro gasps; 'Thanka God. I thought I had a CRACK in my $300 Boccelli leather shoes!'

53.

A police officer stops a blonde for speeding and asks her very nicely if he could see her licence.

She replied in a huff; 'I wish you guys would get your act together. Just yesterday you take away my licence and then today you expect me to show it to you!'

54.

The husband leans over and asks his wife; 'Do you remember the first time we had sex together over 50 years ago? We went behind this very tavern where you leaned against the back fence and I made love to you.'

'Yes', she says. 'I remember it well.'

'OK,' he says. 'How about taking a stroll around there again and we can do it for old time's sake?'

'Oh Charlie, you old devil, that sounds like a crazy, but good idea!'

There's a police officer sitting in the next booth listening to all this, and having a chuckle to himself he thinks; 'I'd better keep an eye on them so there's no trouble.'

So he follows them.

They walk haltingly along, leaning on each other for support aided by walking sticks. Finally they get to the back of the tavern and make their way to the fence. The old lady lifts her skirt and the old man drops his trousers. As she leans against the fence, the old man moves in. Suddenly they erupt into the most furious sex the policeman has ever seen.

This goes on for about ten minutes. Both are making loud noises and moaning and screaming. Finally, they both collapse, panting on the ground.

The policeman is amazed. He thinks he has learned something about life and old age that he didn't know.

After about half an hour of lying on the ground recovering, the old couple struggle to their feet and put their clothes back on. The policeman, still watching, thinks this was truly amazing. He thinks, I've got to ask them what their secret is.

As the couple passes, he says to them; 'Excuse me, but that was something else. You must've had a fantastic sex life together. Is there some sort of secret to this?'

The old man says; '50 years ago that was not an electric fence!'

55.

Two blondes walk into a building . . . you'd think at least one of them would have seen it.

56.

Phone answering machine message; 'If you want to buy marijuana, press the hash key.'

57.

A guy walks into the psychiatrist wearing only Clingwrap for shorts.

The shrink says; 'Well, I can clearly see you're nuts.'

58.

I went to a seafood disco last week and pulled a muscle.

Q: Who was the only Father and son combination to play test cricket?

A: ME and DAD ... Javid Meandad.

Q: Why is Andrew Flintoff the unluckiest of all English cricketers?

A: Because he was born in England.

Q: What is the height of optimism?

A: An English batsman applying sunscreen.

Q: What does Ashley Giles put in his hands to make sure the next ball almost always takes a wicket?

A: A bat.

Q: What would Glen McGrath be if he was an Englishman?

A: An allrounder.

Q: What advantage do Kevin Pietersen, Andrew Strauss and Geraint Jones have over the rest of their team-mates?

A: At least they can say they're not really English.

Q: What is the English version of a hat-trick?

A: Three runs in three balls.

Q: What do you call an Englishman with 100 runs against his name?

A: A bowler.

60.

My friend drowned in a bowl of muesli. A strong currant pulled him in.

61.

A man came round in hospital after a serious accident.

He shouted; 'Doctor, doctor, I can't feel my legs!'

The doctor replied; 'Of course you can't, I've cut your arms off.'

62.

I went to the butcher the other day and I bet him $50 that he couldn't reach the meat off the top shelf. He said; 'No, the steaks are too high.'

63.

Two Eskimos sitting in a kayak were chilly. They lit a fire in the craft, it sank. Proving once and for all that you can't have your kayak and heat it.

64.

Clinton, Bush, and Washington . . .

Bill Clinton, George Bush and George Washington were on the Titanic.

As the boat was sinking, George Washington heroically shouts, 'Save the women!'

George Bush hysterically screeches, 'Screw the women!'

And Bill Clinton's eyes light up and he says, 'Do we have time?'

65.

A man takes his German Shepherd to the vet.

'My dog's cross-eyed, is there anything you can do for him?'

'Well,' says the vet. 'Let's have a look at him'

So he picks the dog up and examines his eyes, then checks his teeth. Finally, he says; 'I'm going to have to put him down.'

'What? Because he's cross-eyed?'

'No, because he's really heavy.'

66.

Man goes to the doctor, with a strawberry growing out of his head.

Doc says; 'I'll give you some cream to put on it.'

67.

'Doc I can't stop singing *The Green, Green Grass of Home.*'

'That sounds like Tom Jones syndrome.'

'Is it common?'

'It's not unusual.'

68.

Guy goes into the doctor's.

'Doc, I've got a cricket ball stuck up my backside.'

'How's that?'

'Don't you start!!'

69.

Two elephants walk off a cliff . . . boom, boom!

70.

Q: What do you call a fish with no eyes?

A: A fsh.

71.

So I was getting into my car, and this bloke comes up to me and says; 'Can you give me a lift?'

I said; 'Sure! You look great, the world's your oyster, go for it!!'

72.

Apparently, one in five people in the world are Chinese. There are five people in my family, so it must be one of them. It's either my Mum or my Dad, or my older brother Colin, or my younger brother Ho-Cha-Chu.

But I think it's Colin.

73.
Two fat blokes are in a pub. One says to the other; 'Your round.'

The other one says; 'So are you, you fat bastard!'

74.
An eagle was sitting on a tree resting, doing nothing.

A small rabbit saw the eagle and asked him; 'Can I also sit like you and do nothing?'

The eagle answered; 'Sure, why not'

So the rabbit sat on the ground below the eagle and rested.

All of a sudden, a fox appeared, jumped on the rabbit and ate it.

The moral of the story is: To be sitting and doing nothing, you must be sitting very, very high up!

75.
Police arrested two kids yesterday.

One was drinking battery acid,
and the other was eating fireworks.

They charged one and let the
other one off.

ST PATRICK'S DAY

A Scottish man, an Englishman and an Irishman were sitting in a pub discussing the best pubs around. The Englishman says, 'There's a pub in the West Midlands where the landlord buys you a drink for every that you buy.'

The Scot is not impressed and says, 'That's nothing! In the Highlands every time you buy a drink the landlord buys you five.'

At this point the Englishman is fairly impressed. The Irishman, totally unimpressed, says 'That's nothing. In Dublin there's this pub where the landlord buys your drinks all night, and then when the bar shuts he takes you into a room and makes love to you.'

The Scot and Englishman are well impressed and ask if the Irishman goes there a lot. He replies, 'No, but my sister told me about it.'

Having dutifully celebrated St Patrick's Day, a drunken Irishman was arrested for acting suspiciously on a zebra crossing.

After being apprehended he said . . . 'I'll play that bloody piano if it kills me.'

77.

You know, somebody actually complimented me on my driving today. They left a little note on the windscreen.

It said; 'Parking Fine.'

So that was nice.

78.

A man walked into the doctors, he said; 'I've hurt my arm in several places.'

The doctor said; 'Well don't go there anymore.'

79.

Ireland's worst air disaster occurred early this morning when a small two-seater Cessna plane crashed into a cemetery.

Irish search and rescue workers have recovered 1826 bodies so far and expect that number to climb as digging continues into the night.

80.

There's this blonde out for a walk. She comes to a river and sees another blonde on the opposite bank. 'Yoo-hoo!' she shouts. 'How can I get to the other side?'

The second blonde looks up the river then down the river and shouts back; 'Hellooo, you ARE on the other side.'

81.

A little bird was flying south for the winter. It was so cold the bird froze and fell to the ground into a large field. While he was lying there, a cow came by and dropped some dung on him. As the frozen bird lay there in the pile of cow dung, he began to realise how warm he was. The dung was actually thawing him out! He lay there all warm and happy, and soon began to sing for joy.

A passing cat heard the bird singing and came to investigate. Following the sound, the cat discovered the bird under the pile of cow dung, and promptly dug him out and ate him.

The moral of the story is:

1) Not everyone who shits on you is your enemy;

2) Not everyone who gets you out of the shit is your friend, and

3) When you're in deep shit, it's best to keep your mouth shut!

82.

You have two choices in life; You can stay single and be miserable, or get married and wish you were dead.

83.

9 ways to know if you have 'Estrogen issues' :

1. Everyone around you has an attitude problem.

2. You're adding chocolate chips to your cheese omelette.

3. The dryer has shrunk every last pair of your jeans.

4. Your husband is suddenly agreeing to everything you say.

5. Everyone's head looks like an invitation to batting practice.

6. Everyone seems to have just landed here from 'outer space'.

7. You can't believe they don't make a tampon bigger than Super Plus.

8. You're sure that everyone is scheming to drive you crazy.

9. The Panadol bottle is empty and you bought it yesterday.

84.

At a cocktail party, one woman said to another; 'Aren't you wearing your wedding ring on the wrong finger?'

'Yes I am. I married the wrong man.'

85.

A lady inserted an ad in the classifieds; 'Husband Wanted'.

Next day, she received a hundred letters. They all said the same thing; 'You can have mine.'

86.

When another woman steals your husband, there is no better revenge than to let her keep him.

87.

A woman is incomplete until she is married. Then she is finished.

88.

A little boy asked his father; 'Daddy, how much does it cost to get married?'

Father replied; 'I don't know son, I'm still paying.'

89.

Marriage is the triumph of imagination over intelligence.

90.

A young son asked; 'Dad, is it true that in some parts of Africa a man doesn't know his wife until he marries her?'

Dad replied; 'That happens in every country, son.'

APRIL FOOL'S DAY

It's the summer of 1957 and Harold goes to pick up his date, Peggy Sue. Harold's a pretty hip guy with his own car and a duck tail hairdo. When he goes to the front door, Peggy Sue's mother answers and invites him in.

'Peggy Sue's not ready yet, so why don't you have a seat?' she says.

That's cool. Peggy Sue's mother asks Harold what they're planning to do. Harold replies politely that they will probably just go to the ice cream shop or to a drive-in movie.

Peggy Sue's mother responds; 'Why don't you kids go out and screw? I hear all the kids are doing it.'

Naturally this comes as quite a surprise to Harold and he says; 'Whaaaat?'

'Yeah,' says Peggy Sue's mother. 'We know Peggy Sue really likes to screw. Why, she'd screw all night if we let her!'

Harold's eyes light up and he smiles from ear to ear. Immediately, he has revised the plans for the evening. A few minutes later, Peggy Sue comes downstairs in her little poodle skirt with her saddle shoes, and announces that she's ready to go.

Almost breathless with anticipation, Harold escorts his date out the front door while Mum is saying; 'Have a good evening kids.' With a small wink for Harold.

About 20 minutes later, a thoroughly dishevelled Peggy Sue rushes back into the house, slams the door behind her and screams at her mother; 'Dammit, Mum! The Twist! The Twist! It's called the Twist!!!'

92.

Then there was a woman who said; 'I never knew what real happiness was until I got married, and by then, it was too late.'

93.

Great truths that little children have learned

* No matter how hard you try, you can't baptise cats.

* When your Mum is mad at your Dad, don't let her brush your hair.

* If your sister hits you, don't hit her back. They always catch the second person.

* Never ask your 3-year old brother to hold a tomato.

* You can't trust dogs to watch your food.

* Don't sneeze when someone is cutting your hair.

* Never hold a Dust-Buster and a cat at the same time.

* You can't hide a piece of broccoli in a glass of milk.

* Don't wear polka-dot underwear under white shorts.

* The best place to be when you're sad is Grandpa's lap.

94.

If you want your spouse to listen and pay strict attention to every word you say . . . talk in your sleep.

95.

Just think, if it weren't for marriage, men would go through life thinking they had no faults at all.

96.

First guy says; 'My wife's an angel!'

Second guy remarks; 'You're lucky, mine's still alive.'

97.

Husband and wife are waiting at the bus stop with their nine children. A blind man joins them after a few minutes.

When the bus arrives, they find it overloaded and only the wife and the nine kids are able to fit onto the bus. So the husband and the blind man decide to walk.

After a while, the husband gets irritated by the ticking of the stick of the blind man as he taps it on the sidewalk, and says to him; 'Why don't you put a piece of rubber at the end of your stick? That ticking sound is driving me crazy.'

The blind man replies; 'If you would've put a rubber at the end of YOUR stick, we'd be riding the bus, so shut the hell up.'

98.

Great truths that adults have learned

* Raising teenagers is like nailing jelly to a tree.

* Wrinkles don't hurt.

* Families are like fudge . . . mostly sweet, with a few nuts.

* Today's mighty oak is just yesterday's nut that held its ground.

* Laughing is good exercise. It's like jogging on the inside.

* Middle age is when you choose your cereal for the fiber, not the toy.

99.

SUCCESS

At age 4 success is . . . *not piddling in your pants.*

At age 12 success is . . . *having friends.*

At age 18 success is . . . *having a driver's licence.*

At age 35 success is . . . *having money.*

At age 50 success is . . . *having money.*

At age 70 success is . . . *having a driver's licence.*

At age 75 success is . . . *having friends.*

At age 80 success is . . . *not piddling in your pants.*

100.

A turkey was chatting with a bull.

'I would love to be able to get to the top of that tree,' sighed the turkey. 'But I haven't got the energy.'

'Well, why don't you nibble on some of my droppings?' replied the bull. 'They're packed with nutrients.'

The turkey pecked at a lump of dung, and found it actually gave him enough strength to reach the lowest branch of the tree.

The next day, after eating some more dung, he reached the second branch.

Finally after a fourth night, the turkey was proudly perched at the top of the tree.

He was promptly spotted by a farmer, who shot him out of the tree.

The moral of the story is: Bullshit might get you to the top, but it won't keep you there.

101.

Two drovers standing in a bar. One asked the other; 'What are you up to?'

'Ahh. I'm takin' a heard of 6000 cattle from Goondiwindi to Gympie.'

'Oh yeah. And what route are you takin'?'

'Ah, prob'ly the Missus . . . after all, she's stuck by me durin' the drought.'

102.

To commemorate her 69th birthday on October 1, 2006 actress/vocalist, Julie Andrews made a special appearance at Manhattan's Radio City Music Hall for a benefit concert.

One of the musical numbers she performed was *My Favorite Things* from the legendary movie *Sound of Music*.

Here are the lyrics she used;

> *Maalox and nose drops and needles for knitting,*
>
> *Walkers and handrails and new dental fittings,*
>
> *Bundles of magazines tied up in string,*
>
> *These are a few of my favorite things.*

Cadillacs and cataracts and hearing aids and glasses,

Polident and Fixodent and false teeth in glasses,

Pacemakers, golf carts and porches with swings,

These are a few of my favorite things.

When the pipes leak,

When the bones creak,

When the knees go bad,

I simply remember my favorite things,

And then I don't feel so bad.

Hot tea and crumpets and corn pads for bunions,

No spicy hot food or food cooked with onions,

Bathrobes and heating pads and hot meals they bring,

These are a few of my favorite things.

Back pains, confused brains, and no need for sinnin',

Thin bones and fractures and hair that is thinnin',

And we won't mention our short shrunken frames,

When we remember our favorite things.

When the joints ache,

When the hips break,

When the eyes grow dim,

Then I remember the great life I've had,

And then I don't feel so bad.

103.

I recently visited a new doctor. After two visits to the GP and exhaustive lab tests, he said I was doing 'fairly well' for my age.

A little concerned about that comment, I couldn't resist asking him; 'Do you think I'll live to be 80?'

He asked; 'Do you smoke tobacco, or drink beer or wine?'

'Oh no,' I replied. 'I'm not doing drugs, either.'

Then he asked; 'Do you eat rib-eye steaks and barbecued ribs?

I said; 'No, my former doctor said that red meat is very unhealthy!'

'Do you spend a lot of time in the sun, like playing golf, sailing, hiking, or bicycling?'

'No, I don't,' I said.

He asked; 'Do you gamble, drive fast cars, or have a little too much sex?'

'No,' I said. 'I don't do any of those things.'

He looked at me and said; 'Then, why do you give a shit if you live to 80?'

104.

An old nun who was living in a convent next to a Brooklyn construction site noticed the coarse language of the workers and decided to spend some time with them to correct their ways.

She decided she would take her lunch, sit with the workers and talk with them. She put her sandwich in a brown bag and walked over to the spot where the men were eating.

She walked up to the group and with a big smile said; 'Do you men know Jesus Christ?'

They shook their heads and looked at each other.

One of the workers looked up into the steelworks and yelled; 'Anybody up there know Jesus Christ?'

One of the steelworkers yelled down; 'No, why'?

The worker yelled back; 'His wife's here with his lunch.'

105.   **EASTER**

A nun walks into Mother Superior's office and plunks down into a chair. She lets out a sigh heavy with frustration.

'What troubles you, Sister?' asks the Mother Superior. 'I thought Easter Monday was the day you spent with your family.'

'It was,' sighed the Sister. 'And I went to play golf with my brother. We try to play golf as often as we can. You know I was quite a talented golfer before I devoted my life to Christ.'

'I seem to recall that,' the Mother Superior agreed. 'So I take it your day of recreation was not relaxing?'

'Far from it,' snorted the Sister. 'In fact, I even took the Lord's name in vain today!'

'Goodness, Sister!' gasped the Mother Superior, astonished. 'You must tell me all about it!'

'Well, we were on the fifth tee ... and this hole is a monster, Mother – 540 yard Par 5, with a nasty dogleg left and a hidden green ... and I hit the drive of my life. I creamed it. The sweetest swing I ever made. And it's flying straight and true, right along the line I wanted ... and it hits a bird in mid-flight not 100 yards off the tee!'

'Oh my!' commiserated the Mother. 'How unfortunate! But surely that didn't make you blaspheme, Sister!'

'No, that wasn't it,' admitted Sister. 'While I was still trying to fathom what had happened, this squirrel runs out of the woods, grabs my ball and runs off down the fairway!'

'Oh, that would have made me blaspheme!' sympathised Mother.

'But I didn't, Mother Superior!' sobbed the Sister. 'And I was so proud of myself! And while I was pondering whether this was a sign from God, this hawk swoops out of the sky and grabs the squirrel and flies off, with my ball still clutched in his paws!'

'So that's when you cursed,' said the Mother with a knowing smile.

'Nope, that wasn't it either,' cried the Sister, anguished, 'because as the hawk started to fly out of sight, the squirrel started struggling, and the hawk dropped him right there on the green, and the ball popped out of his paws and rolled to about 18 inches from the cup!'

Mother Superior sat back in her chair, folded her arms across her chest, fixed the Sister with a baleful stare and said ...

'You missed the f@#$ing putt, didn't you?'

A man and his extremely uptight and complaining wife were visiting the Holy Land when the wife up and died.

The hospital chaplain said that it would cost $5,000 to send his wife back home or $150 to bury her in the Holy Land. The man said he would have to take her home.

The chaplain was surprised by this answer and asked the man why?

The man answered; 'Many years ago a man died in the Holy Land and three days later, he rose from the dead. I can't take that chance.'

106.

HOW to maintain a healthy level of insanity

* At lunch time, sit in your parked car with sunglasses on and point a hair dryer at passing cars. See if they slow down.

* Page yourself over the intercom. Don't disguise your voice.

* Every time someone asks you to do something, ask if they want fries with that.

* Put your wastepaper bin on your desk and label it 'In.'

* Put decaf in the coffee maker for three weeks. Once everyone has gotten over their caffeine addictions, switch to Espresso.

* In the butt of all your cheques write; 'For smuggling diamonds.'

* Finish all your sentences with; 'In accordance with the Prophecy.'

* Don't use any punctuation.

* As often as possible, skip rather than walk.

* Order a diet water whenever you go out to eat, with a serious face.

* Specify that your drive-through order is 'To Go.'

* Sing along at the Opera.

* Go to a poetry reading and ask why the poems don't rhyme.

* Put mosquito netting around your work area and play tropical sounds all day.

* Five days in advance, tell your friends you can't attend their party because you're not in the mood.

* Have your colleagues address you by your wrestling name, Rock Bottom.

* When the money comes out the ATM scream; 'I won! I won!'

* When leaving the zoo, start running towards the car park yelling; 'Run for your lives, they're loose!'

* Tell your children over dinner; 'Due to the economy, we are going to have to let one of you go.'

* And the final way to keep a healthy level of insanity . . .

107.

A man goes into a chemist shop and asks the pharmacist if he can give him something for hiccups. The pharmacist promptly reaches out and slaps the man's face.

'What the heck did you do that for!?' the man screams.

'Well, you don't have the hiccups anymore do you?'

The man says; 'No I don't, you IDIOT . . . But my wife out in the car still does!'

108.

A blonde was driving home after a game and got caught in a really bad hailstorm. Her car was covered with dents, so the next day she took it to a repair shop. The shop owner saw that she was a blonde, so he decided to have some fun.

He told her to go home and blow into the tail pipe really hard, and all the dents would pop out.

So, the blonde went home, got down on her hands and knees and started blowing into her tailpipe. Nothing happened. So she blew a little harder, and still nothing happened.

Her flatmate, another blonde, came home and said, 'What are you doing?'

The first blonde told her how the repairman had instructed her to blow into the tail pipe in order to get all the dents to pop out.

The flatmate rolled her eyes and said, 'Duh, like hello! You need to roll up the windows first.'

109.

Two confirmed bachelors sat talking. Their conversation drifted from politics to cooking.

'I got a cookbook once,' said the first. 'But I could never do anything with it.'

'Too much fancy cooking in it, eh?' asked the second.

'You said it. Every one of the recipes began the same way. Take a clean dish and . . . '

110.

A drunken man walks into a biker bar, sits down at the bar and orders a drink.

Looking around, he sees three men sitting at a corner table. He gets up, staggers to the table, leans over, looks at the biggest, meanest, biker in the face and says; 'I went by your grandma's house today and I saw her in the hallway buck naked. Man, she is one fine looking woman!'

The biker looks at him and doesn't say a word. His buddies are confused, because he is one bad biker and would fight at the drop of a hat.

The drunk leans on the table again and says; 'I got it on with your grandma and she is good, the best I ever had!'

The biker's buddies are starting to get really mad but the biker still says nothing.

The drunk leans on the table one more time and says; 'I'll tell you something else, boy, your grandma liked it!'

At this point the biker stands up, takes the drunk by the shoulders looks him square in the eyes and says; 'Grandpa. Go home, you're drunk!'

111.
What holds a frog's legs on?

Ribbits.

112.
A young man joined the army and signed up with the paratroopers. He went through the standard training, completed the practice jumps from higher and higher structures, and finally went to take his first jump from an airplane. The next day, he called home to tell his father the news.

'So, did you jump?' asked the father.

'Well, let me tell you what happened,' the son said. 'We got up in the plane, and the sergeant opened up the door and asked for volunteers. About a dozen men got up and just walked out of the plane.'

'Is that when you jumped?' asked his father.

'Uh, no. The sergeant started to grab the other men one at a time and throw them out the door.'

'Did you jump then?' asked his father.

'I'm getting to that. Everyone else had jumped, and I was the last man left on the plane. I told the sergeant that I was too scared to jump.'

He told me to get off the plane or he'd kick my butt.

'So, did you jump?'

'No. He tried to push me out of the plane, but I grabbed onto the door and refused to go. Finally he called over the Jump Master. The Jump Master is this great big guy, about two metres and 120 kilos. He said to me, "Are you gonna jump or not?"

'I said, "No sir, I'm too scared." So the Jump Master pulled down his zipper and took out his you-know-what. I swear, Dad, it was about ten inches long and big around as a baseball bat!

'He said, "Either you jump out that door, or I'm sticking this little baby up your backside."'

'So, then did you jump?' asked his father.

'Well, a little, at first.'

113.
A man was at the country club for his weekly round of golf. He began his round with an eagle on the first hole and a birdie on the second.

On the third hole he had just scored his first ever hole-in-one when his mobile phone rang. It was a doctor notifying him that his wife had just been in a terrible accident and was in a critical condition in intensive care.

The man told the doctor to inform his wife of where he was and that he'd be there as soon as possible. As he hung up he realised he was leaving what was shaping up to be his best ever round of golf. He decided to get in a couple more holes before heading to the hospital.

He ended up playing all 18, finishing his round shooting a personal best of 61, shattering the club record by five strokes and beating his previous best game by more than ten.

He was jubilant. Then he remembered his wife. Feeling guilty he dashed to the hospital. He saw the doctor in the corridor and asked about his wife's condition.

The doctor glared at him and shouted; 'You went ahead and finished your round of golf didn't you? I hope you're proud of yourself! While you were out for the past four hours enjoying yourself at the country club your wife has been languishing in the ICU!

'It's just as well you went ahead and finished that round because it will be more than likely your last! For the rest of her life she will require 'round the clock care. And you'll be her care giver!'

The man was feeling so guilty he broke down and sobbed.

The doctor snickered and said; 'Just messing with you. She's dead. What'd you shoot?'

114.

A man went to a doctor and said; 'Doctor I think I am suffering from cowboys disease.'

The doctor asked; 'Well how long do you think you have had it for?'

The man replied; 'Oh, about a Yeeeeaaaarrrrrrhaaaaaaaah!'

115.

A man and his six-year-old daughter were having breakfast. The daughter turns to her father and asks; 'Dad, where does pooh come from?'

Shocked by this question from his little girl, the father thought for a moment and responded,

'Well you see all this food we are eating, it goes down our throat, into our bellies and comes out as pooh when we go to the toilet.'

The daughter looked shocked at this and when the father asked what was wrong the daughter responded; 'Well, where does Tigger come from then?'

116.

On one of the hottest days on record in Texas, the Lone Ranger and Tonto walked into a bar and sat down to drink a beer.

After a few minutes, a big tall cowboy walked in and said; 'Who owns the big white horse outside?'

The Lone Ranger stood up, hitched his gun belt, and said; 'I do . . . Why?'

The cowboy looked at the Lone Ranger and said; 'Just thought you'd like to know that your horse is about dead from the heat.'

The Lone Ranger and Tonto rushed outside and, sure enough, Silver was ready to die from heat exhaustion. The Lone Ranger got the horse some water and soon Silver was starting to feel a little better.

The Lone Ranger turned to Tonto and said; 'Tonto, I want you to run around Silver and see if you can create enough of a breeze to make him start to feel better.'

Tonto said; 'Yes, Kemosabe,' and took off running circles around Silver.

Not able to do anything else but wait, the Lone Ranger returned to the bar to finish his drink. A few minutes later, another cowboy struts into the bar and asks; 'Who owns that big white horse outside?'

The Lone Ranger stands again, and claims; 'I do, what's wrong with him this time?'

The cowboy looks him in the eye and says; 'Nothing, but you left your Injun runnin'.'

117.

A wife was making a breakfast of fried eggs for her husband. Suddenly, her husband burst into the kitchen.

'Careful,' he said. 'CAREFUL! Put in some more butter! Oh my GOD! You're cooking too many at once. TOO MANY! Turn them! TURN THEM NOW! We need more butter. Oh my GOD! WHERE are we going to get MORE BUTTER? They're going to STICK! Careful. CAREFUL! I said be CAREFUL! You NEVER listen to me when you're cooking! Never! Turn them! Hurry up! Are you CRAZY? Have you LOST your mind? Don't forget to salt them. You know you always forget to salt them. Use the salt. USE THE SALT! THE SALT!'

The wife stared at him; 'What in the world is wrong with you? You think I don't know how to fry a couple of eggs?'

The husband calmly replied; 'I just wanted to show you what it feels like when I'm driving.'

118.
Two birds were sitting on a Perch. One bird turned to the other and said; 'Can you smell fish?'

119.
Two fish are sitting in a tank. One says to the other; 'Can you drive this thing?'

120.
A man walks into a pharmacy with his 8-year old son.

They happen to walk by the condom display, and the boy asks; 'What are these, Dad?'

To which the man matter-of-factly replies; 'Those are called condoms, son. Men use them to have safe sex.'

'Oh I see,' replied the boy pensively. 'Yes, I've heard of that in health class at school.'

He looks over the display and picks up a pack of three and asks; 'Why are there three in this package?'

The dad replies; 'Those are for university boys. One for Friday, one for Saturday, and one for Sunday.'

'Cool,' says the boy.

He notices a six-pack and asks; 'Then who are these for?'

'Those are for bachelors,' the dad answers. 'Two for Friday, two for Saturday and two for Sunday.'

'WOW!' exclaimed the boy.

'Then who uses THESE?' he asks, picking up a 12-pack.

With a sigh and a tear in his eye, the dad replied; 'Those are for married men. ONE for January, ONE for February, ONE for March . . .'

121.

A judge enters the courtroom, strikes the gavel and says; 'Before I begin this trial, I have an announcement to make. The lawyer for the defence has paid me $15,000 to swing the case his way. The lawyer for the plaintiff has paid me $10,000 to swing the case her way.

'In order to make this a fair trial, I am returning $5,000 to the defence.'

122.

TO My Dear Wife

During the past year I have tried to make love to you 365 times.

I have succeeded 36 times, which is an average of once every ten days.

The following is a list of why I did not succeed more often;

54 times the sheets were clean

17 times it was too late

49 times you were too tired

20 times it was too hot

15 times you pretended to be asleep

22 times you had a headache

17 times you were afraid of waking the baby

16 times you said you were too sore

12 times it was the wrong time of the month

19 times you had to get up early

9 times you said you weren't in the mood

7 times you were sunburned

6 times you were watching the late show

5 times you didn't want to mess up your new hairdo

3 times you said the neighbours would hear us

9 times you said your mother would hear us

Of the 36 times I did succeed, the activity was not satisfactory because;

6 times you just laid there

8 times you reminded me there's a crack in the ceiling

4 times you told me to hurry up and get it over with

7 times I had to wake you and tell you I finished

1 time I was afraid I had hurt you because I felt you move

TO MY Dear HUSBAND

I think you have things a little confused. Here are the reasons you didn't get more than you did;

5 times you came home drunk and tried to screw the cat

36 times you did not come home at all

21 times you didn't come

33 times you came too soon

19 times you went soft before you got in

38 times you worked too late

10 times you got cramps in your toes

29 times you had to get up early to play golf

2 times you were in a fight and someone kicked you in the balls

4 times you got it stuck in your zipper

3 times you had a cold and your nose was running

2 times you had a splinter in your finger

20 times you lost the notion after thinking about it all day

6 times you came in your pyjamas while reading a dirty book

98 times you were too busy watching TV

Of the times we did get together;

The reason I laid still was because you missed and were screwing the sheets.

I wasn't talking about the crack in the ceiling, what I said was; 'Would you prefer me on my back or kneeling?'

The time you felt me move was because you farted and I was trying to breathe.

123.

The old man in his mid-80s struggles to get up from the couch then starts putting on his coat. His wife, seeing the unexpected behavior, asks; 'Where are you going?'

He replies; 'I'm going to the doctor.'

She says; 'Why, are you sick?'

He says; 'Nope, I'm going to get me some of that Viagra stuff.'

Immediately the wife starts working and positioning herself to get out of her rocker and begins to put on her coat.

He says; 'Where the hell are you going'?

She answers; 'I'm going to the doctor, too.'

He says; 'Why, what do you need?'

She says; 'If you're going to start using that rusty old thing, I'm getting a tetanus shot.'

In a tiny village on the Irish coast lived an old lady, a virgin and very proud of it.

Sensing that her final days were rapidly approaching, and desiring to make sure everything was in proper order when she dies, she went to the town's undertaker (who also happened to be the local postal clerk) to make proper 'final' arrangements.

As a last wish, she informed the undertaker that she wanted the following inscription engraved on her tombstone; BORN A VIRGIN, LIVED AS A VIRGIN, DIED A VIRGIN

Not long after, the old maid died peacefully.

A few days after the funeral, as the undertaker-postal clerk went to prepare the tombstone that the lady had requested, it became quite apparent that the tombstone that she had selected was much too small for the wording that she had chosen.

He thought long and hard about how he could fulfil the old maid's final request, considering the very limited space available on the small piece of stone.

For days, he agonised over the dilemma. But finally his experience as a postal worker allowed him to come up with what he thought was the appropriate solution to the problem.

The virgin's tombstone was finally completed and duly engraved; RETURNED UNOPENED!

125.

A blonde's car breaks down on the motorway one day. So she eases it over onto the shoulder of the road. She carefully steps out of the car and opens the trunk. Out jump two men in trench coats who walk to the rear of the vehicle where they stand facing oncoming traffic and begin opening their coats and exposing their naked bodies to approaching drivers.

Not surprisingly, one of the worst pileups in the history of this highway occurs. It's not very long before a police car shows up.

The cop, clearly enraged, runs toward the blonde of the disabled vehicle yelling; 'What the heck is going on here?'

'My car broke down,' says the blonde calmly.

'Well, what are these perverts doing here by the road?' asks the cop.

And she said; 'Oh, those are my emergency flashers!'

126.

The day finally arrived.

Forrest Gump dies and goes to Heaven. He is at the Pearly Gates, met by St Peter himself. However, the gates are closed, and Forrest approaches the gatekeeper.

St Peter said; 'Well, Forrest, it is certainly good to see you. We have heard a lot about you. I must tell you, though, that the place is filling up fast, and we have been administering an entrance examination for everyone. The test is short, but you have to pass it before you can get into Heaven.'

Forrest responds; 'It sure is good to be here, St Peter, sir. But nobody ever told me about any entrance exam. I sure hope that the test isn't too hard. Life was a big enough test as it was.'

St Peter continued; 'Yes, I know, Forrest, but the test is only three questions.'

'First. What two days of the week begin with the letter T?

Second. How many seconds are there in a year?

Third. What is God's first name?'

Forrest leaves to think the questions over.

He returns the next day and sees St Peter, who waves him up, and says; 'Now that you have had a chance to think the questions over, tell me your answers.'

Forrest replies; 'Well, the first one . . . which two days in the week begins with the letter T? Shucks, that one is easy. That would be Today and Tomorrow.'

The Saint's eyes opened wide and he exclaimed; 'Forrest that is not what I was thinking but you do have a point and, I guess, I did not specify so I will give you credit for that answer. How about the next one?'

'How many seconds in a year? Now that one is harder,' replied Forrest. 'But I thunk and thunk about that, and I guess the only answer can be 12.'

Astounded, St Peter said; 'Twelve? Twelve? Forrest, how in Heaven's name could you come up with 12 seconds in a year?'

Forrest replied; 'Shucks, there's got to be 12; January 2nd, February 2nd, March 2nd . . . '

'Hold it,' interrupts St Peter. 'I see where you are going with this and I see your point though that was not quite what I had in mind. But I will have to give you credit for that one, too. Let us go on with the third and final question. Can you tell me God's first name'?

'Sure,' Forrest replied. 'It's Andy.'

'Andy?' exclaimed an exasperated and frustrated St Peter.

'Ok, I can understand how you came up with your answers to my first two questions, but just how in the world did you come up with the name Andy as the first name of God?'

'Shucks, that was the easiest one of all,' Forrest replied. 'I learnt it from the song, 'Andy walks with me, Andy talks with me, Andy tells me I am his own . . . '

St Peter opened the Pearly Gates, and said; 'Run Forrest. Run!'

127.

A man is driving along a highway and sees a rabbit jump out across the middle of the road.

He swerves to avoid hitting it, but unfortunately the rabbit jumps right in front of the car.

The driver, a sensitive man as well as an animal lover, pulls over and gets out to see what has become of the rabbit. Much to his dismay, the rabbit is dead.

The driver feels so awful that he begins to cry.

A beautiful blonde woman driving down the highway sees the man crying on the side of the road and pulls over.

She steps out of the car and asks the man what's wrong.

'I feel terrible,' he explains. 'I accidentally hit this rabbit and killed it.'

The blonde says; 'Don't worry.'

She runs to her car and pulls out a spray can. She walks over to the limp, dead rabbit, bends down, and sprays the contents onto the rabbit.

The rabbit jumps up, waves its paw at the two of them and hops off down the road.

Two metres away the rabbit stops, turns around and waves again. He hops down the road another two metres, turns and waves. Hops another two metres, turns and waves, and repeats this again and again and again, until he hops out of sight.

The man is astonished.

He runs over to the woman and demands; 'What is in that can? What did you spray on that rabbit?'

The woman turns the can around so that the man can read the label.

It says; 'Hair Spray . . . Restores life to dead hair, and adds permanent wave.'

128. Two hydrogen atoms meet. One says; 'I've lost my electron.'

The other says; 'Are you sure?'

The first replies; 'Yes, I'm positive.'

129. In the beginning, God covered the earth with broccoli, cauliflower and spinach, combined with an abundance of green, yellow and red vegetables. He did this so that Man and Woman would live long and healthy lives.

Then, using God's bountiful gifts, Satan created Dairy Whip and Peter's Ice Cream.

And Satan said; 'You want hot fudge with that?'

And Man said; 'Yes!'

And Woman said; 'I'll have one too . . . with sprinkles.'

And lo and behold, they gained five kilos.

So God created the healthful yoghurt that Woman might keep the figure that Man found so fair.

So Satan brought forth white flour from the wheat, and sugar from the cane, and combined them. And Woman went from size 12 to size 14.

So God said; 'Try my fresh green garden salad.'

So Satan presented crumbled Blue Cheese dressing and garlic toast on the side. And Man and Woman unfastened their belts following the repast.

God then said; 'I have sent you heart-healthy vegetables and olive oil in which to cook them.'

So Satan brought forth deep-fried calamari, butter-dipped lobster chunks, and fried chicken so big it needed its own platter.

And Man's cholesterol sharply increased.

Then God brought forth the potato, naturally low in fat and brimming with potassium and good nutrition.

Then Satan peeled off the healthy skin, sliced the starchy centre into chips and deep-fried them in animal fats adding copious quantities of salt.

And Man packed on more kilos.

God then brought forth running shoes so that his children might lose those extra pounds.

So Satan introduced cable TV with remote control so Man would not have to toil changing the channels. And Man and Woman laughed and cried before the flickering light and started wearing stretchy lycra jogging suits.

God then gave lean beef so that Man might consume fewer calories and still satisfy his appetite.

Satan created McDonald's and the double cheeseburger.

Then Satan said; 'You want fries with that?'

And Man replied; 'Yes! And super size them!'

And Satan said, 'It is good.'

And Man and Woman went into cardiac arrest.

God sighed and created quadruple by-pass surgery.

Satan chuckled and created the Public Health System!!!

130.

A man walked into the ladies' section of a Department Store and said to the woman behind the counter; 'I'd like to buy a Baptist bra for my wife, size 36B.'

'What type of bra?' asked the assistant.

'Baptist,' said the man. 'She said get a Baptist bra and that you'd know what she meant.'

'Ah yes, now I remember,' said the saleslady. 'We don't sell many of those. Mostly our customers want the Catholic type, the Salvation Army type, or the Presbyterian type.'

Confused, the man asked; 'What's the difference between them?'

The lady responded; 'It is all really quite simple.'

'The Catholic type supports the masses.

'The Salvation Army type lifts up the fallen.

'And the Presbyterian type keeps them staunch and upright.'

'So what does the Baptist type do?' asked the man.

'Makes mountains out of molehills,' she replied

131. A blonde was playing Trivial Pursuit one night.

It was her turn. She rolled the dice and she landed on Science & Nature.

Her question was; 'If you are in a vacuum and someone calls your name, can you hear it?'

She thought for a time and then asked; 'Is it on or off?'

132.
A vulture boards a plane with two dead raccoons. The stewardess looks at him and says; 'I'm sorry, sir, only one carrion allowed per passenger.'

133.
Did you hear about the Buddhist who refused Novocain during a root canal?

His goal: To transcend dental medication.

134.
A couple has twins and gives them up for adoption.

One goes to a family in Egypt and is named Ahmal.

The other goes to a family in Spain and they name him Juan.

Years later Juan sends a picture of himself to his birth parents.

The mother says; 'I wonder what his brother looks like.'

Her husband replies; 'They're twins! If you've seen Juan, you've seen Ahmal.'

135.
Mahatma Gandhi, as you know, walked barefoot most of the time, which produced an impressive set of calluses on his feet.

He also ate very little, which made him rather frail and with his odd diet, he suffered from bad breath.

This made him . . . A super calloused fragile mystic hexed by halitosis.

136.

MOTHER'S DAY

Why God made moms

Answers given by 2nd grade school children to the following questions:

Why did God make mothers?

1. She's the only one who knows where the scotch tape is.

2. Mostly to clean the house.

3. To help us out of there when we were getting born.

How did God make mothers?

1. He used dirt, just like for the rest of us.

2. Magic plus super powers and a lot of stirring.

3. God made my Mum just the same like he made me. He just used bigger parts.

What ingredients are mothers made of?

1. God makes mothers out of clouds and angel hair and everything nice in the world and one dab of mean.

2. They had to get their start from men's bones. Then they mostly use string, I think.

Why did God give you your mother and not some other mum?

1. We're related.

2. God knew she likes me a lot more than other people's mums like me.

What kind of little girl was your Mum?

1. My Mum has always been my mum and none of that other stuff.

2. I don't know because I wasn't there, but my guess would be pretty bossy.

3. They say she used to be nice.

What did Mum need to know about Dad before she married him?

1. His last name.

2. She had to know his background. Like is he a crook? Does he get drunk on beer?

3. Does he make at least $80,000 a year? Did he say NO to drugs and YES to chores?

Why did your Mum marry your Dad?

1. My Dad makes the best spaghetti in the world. And my Mum eats a lot.

2. She got too old to do anything else with him.

3. My Grandma says that Mum didn't have her thinking cap on.

Who's the boss at your house?

1. Mum doesn't want to be boss, but she has to because Dad's such a goof ball.

2. Mum. You can tell by room inspection. She sees the stuff under the bed.

3. I guess Mum is, but only because she has a lot more to do than Dad.

What's the difference between Mums and Dads?

1. Mums work at work and work at home and Dads just go to work at work.

2. Mums know how to talk to teachers without scaring them.

3. Dads are taller and stronger, but Mums have all the real power 'cause that's who you got to ask if you want to sleep over at your friend's.

4. Mums have magic, they make you feel better without medicine.

What does your Mum do in her spare time?

1. Mothers don't do spare time.

2. To hear her tell it, she pays bills all day long.

What would it take to make your Mum perfect?

1. On the inside she's already perfect. Outside, I think some kind of plastic surgery.

2. Diet. You know, her hair. I'd diet, maybe blue.

If you could change one thing about your Mum, what would it be?

1. She has this weird thing about me keeping my room clean. I'd get rid of that.

2. I'd make my Mum smarter. Then she would know it was my sister who did it and not me.

3. I would like for her to get rid of those invisible eyes on the back of her head.

137.

There was the person who sent ten different puns to friends, with the hope that at least one of the puns would make them laugh.

No pun in ten did.

138.

A Queensland drover was grazing his herd on the long acre along a remote pasture in outback Queensland when suddenly a brand new Range Rover emerged from a dust cloud towards him.

The driver, a young man in an Armani suit, Gucci shoes, Bolle sunglasses and Yves St Laurent silk tie, leans out the window and asks the drover; 'If I tell you exactly how many cows and calves you have in your herd, will you give me a calf?'

The cowboy looks at the man, obviously a yuppie, then looks at his peacefully grazing herd and calmly answers; 'Sure, Why not?'

The yuppie parks his car, whips out his Dell notebook computer, connects it to his Nokia cell phone, and surfs to a NASA page on the Internet, where he calls up a GPS satellite navigation system to get an exact fix on his location which he then feeds to another NASA satellite that scans the area in an ultra-high-resolution photo.

The young man then opens the digital photo in Adobe Photoshop and exports it to an image processing facility in Hamburg, Germany.

Within seconds, he receives an email on his Palm Pilot that the image has been processed and the data stored.

He then accesses a MS-SQL database through an ODBC connected Excel spreadsheet with email on his Blackberry and, after a few minutes, receives a response.

Finally, he prints out a full-color, 150-page report on his hi-tech, miniaturized HP LaserJet printer and finally turns to the cowboy and says; 'You have exactly 1,586 cows and calves.'

'That's right. Well, I guess you can take one of my calves,' says the Cowboy.

He watches the young man select one of the animals and looks on, amused, as the young man stuffs it into the trunk of his car.

Then the cowboy says to the young man; 'Hey, if I can tell you exactly what your business is, will you give me back my calf?'

The young man thinks about it for a second and then says; 'Okay, why not?'

'You're a Parliamentarian from Canberra,' says the drover.

'Wow! That's correct,' says the yuppie, 'but how did you guess that?'

'No guessing required,' answered the drover.

'You showed up here even though nobody called you. You want to get paid for an answer I already knew, to a question I never asked. You tried to show me how much smarter than me you are; and you don't know a thing about cows.

'Now give me back my dog!'

139.

Our ice cream man was found lying on the floor of his van covered with hundreds and thousands. Police say that he topped himself.

140.

A man was walking home alone late one foggy night, when he hears;

BUMP...

BUMP...

BUMP... behind him.

Walking faster, he looks back and through the fog he makes out the image of an upright casket banging its way down the middle of the street toward him.

BUMP...

BUMP...

BUMP...

Terrified, the man begins to run toward his home, the casket bouncing quickly behind him.

Faster...

Faster...

BUMP...

BUMP...

BUMP...

He runs up to his door, fumbles with his keys, opens the door, rushes in, slams and locks the door behind him.

However, the casket crashes through his door, with the lid of the casket clapping.

> *Clappity-BUMP...*
>
> *Clappity-BUMP...*
>
> *Clappity-BUMP...*

On his heels the terrified man runs.

Rushing upstairs to the bathroom, the man locks himself in. His heart is pounding; his head is reeling; his breath is coming in sobbing gasps.

With a loud CRASH the casket breaks down the door.

Bumping and clapping toward him.

The man screams and reaches for something, anything, but all he can find is a bottle of cough syrup!

Desperate, he throws the cough syrup at the casket ... and ...

The coffin stops!!!

141.
 During a Papal audience, a businessman approached the Pope and made this offer; Change the last line of the Lord's Prayer from 'Give us this day our daily bread' to 'Give us this day our daily chicken' and KFC will donate $10 million dollars to Catholic charities.

The Pope declined.

Two weeks later the man approached the Pope again. This time with a $50 million offer.

Again the Pope declined.

A month later the man offers $100 million. This time the Pope accepts.

At a meeting of the Cardinals, the Pope announces his decision in the good news/bad news format.

'The good news is that we have $100 million for charities. The bad news is that we lost the Tip Top account!'

142.
Hello, and welcome to the Psychiatric Hotline.

If you are obsessive-compulsive, please press 1 repeatedly.

If you are co-dependent, please ask someone to press 2.

If you have multiple personalities, please press 3, 4, 5 and 6.

If you are paranoid-delusional . . .

143.
Why are seagulls called seagulls?

Because if they flew over the bay they'd be called bagels!

144.
Q: How many psychiatrists does it take to change a light bulb?

A: Only one, but the light bulb has to WANT to change.

145.

If you pull the wings off of a fly, does it become a walk?

146.

Three convicts escape from prison. They make it to a nearby town but are confronted by a policeman.

'Hey, aren't you those three escaped convicts?' asked the policeman.

Thinking on his feet the first convict looked around him and said; 'No, I'm Mark, Mark Spencer.'

The second followed his lead and said; 'My names is William, W H Smith.'

The third said; 'My name is Ken . . . TuckyFriedChicken.'

147.

Q: What did the Zen-master say to the New York City hotdog vendor?

A: Make me one with everything.

148.

President Clinton is out jogging, and he encounters a man with some puppies.

Clinton asks the man what kind of puppies they are, and the man responds; 'They're Democrat puppies, Mr. President.'

Clinton thinks that is so great that the next day he brings the first lady to see these puppies for herself.

KOChie's Best JOKes 2

He asks the man to tell Hillary what kind of puppies they are, and the man responds; 'They're Republican puppies.'

The President looks puzzled and says; 'Yesterday, you told me they were Democrat puppies.'

The man smiles and says; 'Yesterday, they were. But today, they have their eyes open!'

149.

Your dog's barking at the back door.

Your wife's barking at the front.

Who do you let in first?

Well, it's your call . . . but the dog will stop barking when you let him in.

150.

Why is 6 afraid of 7?

Because 7 ate 9

151.

One night, the Potato family sat down to dinner. Mother Potato, Father Potato and their three daughters. Midway through the meal, the eldest daughter spoke up.

'Mother Potato,' she said. 'I have an announcement to make.'

'And what might that be?' said Mother, seeing the obvious excitement in her eldest daughter's eyes.

'Well,' replied the daughter, with a proud but sheepish grin. 'I'm getting married!'

The other daughters squealed with surprise as Mother Potato exclaimed; 'Married! That's wonderful! And who are you marrying, Eldest daughter?'

'I'm marrying a Russet!'

'A Russet!' replied Mother Potato with pride. 'Oh, a Russet is a fine tater, a fine tater indeed!'

As the family shared in the eldest daughter's joy, the middle daughter spoke up; 'Mother, I too have an announcement.'

'And what might that be?' encouraged Mother Potato.

Not knowing quite how to begin, the middle daughter paused, then said with conviction; 'I too am getting married!'

'You, too!' Mother Potato said with joy. 'That's wonderful! Twice the good news in one evening! And who are you marrying, Middle Daughter?'

'I'm marrying an Idaho!' beamed the middle daughter.

'An Idaho!' said Mother Potato with joy. 'Oh, an Idaho is a fine tater, a fine tater indeed!'

Once again, the room came alive with laughter and excitement to plan for the future, when the youngest Potato daughter interrupted.

'Mother? Mother Potato? Um, I, too, have an announcement to make.'

'Yes?' said Mother Potato with great anticipation.

'Well,' began the youngest Potato daughter with the same sheepish grin as her older sister before her. 'I hope this doesn't come as a shock to you, but I am getting married, as well!'

'Really?' said Mother Potato with sincere excitement.

'All of my lovely daughters married! What wonderful news! And who, pray tell, are you marrying, Youngest Daughter?'

'I'm marrying Bruce McAveney!'

'BRUCE McAVENEY?!' Mother Potato scowled suddenly. 'But he's just a common tater!'

152.

What's the last thing to go through a bug's mind as it hits the windshield?

His arse!

153.

Why were the little strawberries upset?

Because their parents were in a jam.

154.

A Jewish man walks into a bar and sits down. He has a few drinks, then he sees a Chinese man and punches him in the face.

'Ouch!' the Chinese man says. 'What was that for?'

'That was for Pearl Harbor,' the Jewish man says.

'But I'm Chinese!'

'Chinese, Japanese, what's the difference?'

And the Jewish man sits back down. Then, the Chinese man walks up to the Jewish man and punches him in the face.

'Ouch!' the Jewish man says. 'What was that for?'

'That was for the Titanic,' the Chinese man says.

'But that was an iceberg!'

'Iceberg, Goldberg, what's the difference?'

A man sits down at a restaurant and looks at the menu.

He tells the waiter; 'I think I will have the turtle soup.'

The waiter leaves, but the man changes his mind to pea soup.

He yells to the waiter; 'Hold the turtle, make it pea.'

Great truths about Growing Old

* Growing old is mandatory; growing up is optional.

* Forget the health food. I need all the preservatives I can get.

* When you fall down, you wonder what else you can do while you're down there.

* You're getting old when you get the same sensation from a rocking chair that you once got from a roller coaster.

* It's frustrating when you know all the answers but nobody bothers to ask you the questions.

★ Time may be a great healer, but it's a lousy beautician.

★ Wisdom comes with age, but sometimes age comes alone.

157.

Hear about the psychic midget who escaped from jail?

Yeah, the headlines in the newspaper read SMALL MEDIUM AT LARGE.

158.

Billy was at school and the teacher asked all the children what their fathers did for a living. All the typical answers came out; fireman, policeman, salesman, chippy, captain of industry etc.

But Billy was being uncharacteristically quiet so the teacher asked him about his father.

'My father is an exotic dancer in a gay club and takes off all his clothes in front of other men. Sometimes if the offer is really good, he'll go out with a man, rent a cheap hotel room and let them sleep with him.'

The teacher quickly set the other children some work and took little Billy aside to ask him if that was really true.

'No,' said Billy. 'He plays cricket for England but I was just too embarrassed to say.'

Q: How many Windows support staff does it take to change a light bulb?

A: Well, we have an exact copy of your bulb here, and it works fine. Did you check your CONFIG.SYS?

CHRISTMAS IN JULY

Two young lovers go up to the mountains for a romantic Christmas in July winter vacation. When they get there, the guy goes out to chop some wood. When he gets back, he says, 'Honey, my hands are freezing!'

She says, 'Well put them here between my legs and that will warm them up.'

After lunch he goes back out to chop some more wood and comes back and again says, 'Man! My hands are really freezing!'

She says again, 'Well put them here between my legs and warm them up.'

He does, and again that warms him up.

After dinner, he goes out one more time to chop wood for the night.

When he returns, he again says, 'Honey, my hands are really freezing!'

She looks at him and says, 'For crying out loud, don't your ears ever get cold?!!'

1̄61.

John the farmer was in the fertilized egg business. He had several hundred young layers (hens), called 'pullets', and ten roosters whose job it was to fertilize the eggs (for you city folks).

The farmer kept records and any rooster that didn't perform went into the soup pot and was replaced. That took an awful lot of his time, so he bought a set of tiny bells and attached them to his roosters.

Each bell had a different tone so John could tell from a distance, which rooster was performing. Now he could sit on the porch and fill out an efficiency report simply by listening to the bells.

The farmer's favorite rooster was Old Butch, and a very fine specimen he was, too. But on this particular morning John noticed Old Butch's bell hadn't rung at all!

John went to investigate.

The other roosters were chasing pullets, bells-a-ringing. The pullets, hearing the roosters coming, would run for cover. But to Farmer John's amazement, Old Butch had his bell in his beak, so it couldn't ring.

He'd sneak up on a pullet, do his job and walk on to the next one.

John was so proud of Old Butch, he entered him in the Renfrew County Fair and he became an overnight sensation among the judges.

The result . . . The judges not only awarded old Butch the No-Bell Piece Prize but they also awarded him the Pulletsurprise as well. Clearly Old Butch was a politician in the making; who else but a politician could figure out how to win two of the most highly coveted awards on our planet by being the best at sneaking up on the populace and screwing them when they weren't paying attention.

162.

A very loud, unattractive, hard-faced woman walks into Big W with her two kids in tow, screaming obscenities at them all the way through the entrance.

The assistant on the door says; 'Good morning and welcome to Big W. Nice children you've got there . . . are they twins?'

The fat ugly woman stops screaming long enough to snarl; 'Of course they bloody aren't! The oldest, he's nine and the younger one, she's seven. Why the hell would you think they're twins? Do you really think they look alike, ya dickead?'

'Absolutely not,' replies the assistant. 'I just can't believe anyone would shag you twice!'

163.

Two blokes are pushing their shopping trolleys around a supermarket when they collide.

The first bloke says to the second bloke; 'Sorry about that. I'm looking for my wife, and I guess I wasn't paying attention to where I was going.'

The second bloke says; 'That's OK. It's a coincidence. I'm looking for my wife, too. I can't find her and I'm getting a little desperate.'

The first bloke says; 'Well, maybe we can help each other. What does your wife look like?'

The second bloke says; 'Well, she is 26, 5 feet 11, with blonde hair, blue eyes, big jubblies, long legs and is wearing tiny little shorts and a crop top. What does your wife look like?'

The first bloke says; 'Doesn't matter, let's look for yours!'

164.

Two old couples sit down to lunch at a nursing home.

One of the men says to the other; 'What did you do yesterday?'

The man replies; 'We went to the movies?'

'What did you see?'

'Ummm . . . what's that flower with a strong smell and thorns?'

'A rose.'

'Rose, what did we see at the movies yesterday?'

165.

A teenage granddaughter comes downstairs for her date with this see-through blouse on and no bra.

Her grandmother just had a fit, telling her not to dare go out like that!

The teenager tells her; 'Loosen up Grams. These are modern times. You gotta let your rose buds show!'

And then she goes out.

The next day the teenager comes downstairs, and the grandmother is sitting there with no top on.

The teenager wants to die. She explains to her grandmother that she has friends coming over and that it is just not appropriate.

The grandmother says; 'Loosen up, sweetie. If you can show off your rose buds, then I can display my hanging baskets. Happy Gardening.'

166.

Murphy calls to see his mate Paddy who has a broken leg.

Paddy says; 'Me feet are freezing mate, could you nip upstairs and get me slippers?'

'No bother,' he says and he runs upstairs and there are Paddy's two stunning 19-year-old twin daughters sitting on their beds.

'Hello dere girls, your Da' sent me up here to shag ya both.'

'Fook off you liar!'

'I'll prove it,' Murphy says.

So he shouts down the stairs; 'Both of them, Paddy?'

'Of course, what's the use of fookin' one?'

167.

At a U2 concert in Glasgow, Bono asked the audience for some quiet. Then in the silence, he started to slowly clap his hands.

Holding the audience in total silence, he said into the microphone.

'Every time I clap my hands, a child in Africa dies.'

A voice from near the front pierced the silence; 'Well, stop fricken' clapping then!'

168.

Melbourne Zoo had acquired a female of a very rare species of gorilla. Within a few weeks, the gorilla became very cantankerous and difficult to handle.

Upon examination, the zoo veterinarian determined the problem. The gorilla was on heat.

To make matters worse, there were no male gorillas of the species available.

While reflecting on their problem the zoo management noticed Rick, a big Kiwi lad, responsible for fixing the zoo's machinery. Rick, like most Kiwis, had little sense but seemed to be possessed with ample ability to satisfy the female of any species.

So, the zoo administrators thought they might have a solution. Rick was approached with a proposition.

Would he be willing to have sex with the gorilla for $500? Rick showed some interest, but said he would have to think the matter over carefully.

The following day, Rick announced that he would accept their offer, but only under three conditions.

'First,' he said. 'I don't want to have to kuss er.'

'Sicondly, you must niver tull anyone about thus.'

The zoo administration quickly agreed to these conditions, then asked what was his third condition.

'Wull,' said Rick. 'You gotta give me another wik to come up with the $500.'

169.

A rather confident young man walks into a bar and takes a seat next to a very attractive young woman. He gives her a quick glance, then casually looks at his watch for a moment.

The woman notices this and asks, 'Is your date running late?'

'No,' he replies, 'I just bought this state-of-the-art watch and I was testing it.'

Intrigued, the woman says, 'A state-of-the-art watch? What's so special about it?'

'It uses alpha waves to telepathically talk to me,' he explains.

'What's it telling you now?'

'Well, it says that you're not wearing any panties . . .'

The woman giggles and replies, 'Well it must be broken then, because I am wearing panties!'

The man exclaims, 'Damn – this thing must be an hour fast!'

170.

A man and his wife are dining at a table in a plush restaurant, and the husband keeps staring at a drunken lady swigging her drink as she sits alone at a nearby table.

The wife asks, 'Do you know her?'

'Yes,' sighs the husband. 'She's my ex-girlfriend. I understand she took to drinking right after we split up seven years ago, and I hear she hasn't been sober since.'

'My God!' says the wife. 'Who would think a person could go on celebrating that long?'

171.

Q: Who has the easiest job in the English Cricket squad?

A: The guy who removes the red ball marks from the bats.

172.

Q: What does 'Ashes' stand for?

A: Another Sad Horrific English Series.

173.

Q: Who spends the most time on the crease of anyone in the English team?

A: The person who irons the cricket whites.

174.

EIGHT WORDS WITH TWO MEANINGS

1. THINGY (thing-ee) n.

Female: Any part under a car's hood.

Male: The strap fastener on a woman's bra.

2. VULNERABLE (vul-ne-ra-bel) adj.

Female: Fully opening up oneself emotionally to another.

Male: Playing football without a cup.

3. COMMUNICATION (ko-myoo-ni-kay-shon) n.

Female: The open sharing of thoughts and feelings with one's partner.

Male: Leaving a note before taking off on a fishing trip with the boys.

4. COMMITMENT (ko-mit-ment) n.

Female: A desire to get married and raise a family.

Male: Trying not to hit on other women while out with this one.

5. ENTERTAINMENT (en-ter-tayn-ment) n.

Female: A good movie, concert, play or book.

Male: Anything that can be done while drinking beer.

6. FLATULENCE (flach-u-lens) n.

Female: An embarrassing by-product of indigestion.

Male: A source of entertainment, self-expression and male bonding.

7. MAKING LOVE (may-king luv) n.

Female: The greatest expression of intimacy a couple can achieve.

Male: Call it whatever you want, just as long as we do it.

8. REMOTE CONTROL (ri-moht kon-trohl) n.

Female: A device for changing from one TV channel to another.

Male: A device for scanning through all 375 channels every five minutes.

175.

Q: Why did the duck go to the bank?

A: He needed to pay his bill.

176.

A woman gets on a bus and is disgusted when a little old man stands up to give her his seat.

'Patronising old fool,' she mutters as she pushes him back down.

A minute later another woman gets on and the old man rises to his feet once more.

'Male chauvinist pig,' seethes the woman as she pushes him back down again.

The bus stops again, more women get on, and once more the little old man attempts to stand up.

'You're living in the Stone Age,' hisses the woman as she pushes him down.

'For Heavens sake!' wails the little old man. 'Will you let me get off? I've missed three stops already!'

171.
Paddy's pregnant sister was in a terrible car accident and went into a deep coma. After being in the coma for nearly six months she wakes up and sees that she is no longer pregnant.

Frantically she asks the doctor about her baby. The doctor replies; 'Ma'am, you actually had twins. A boy and a girl. The babies are fine now.

'However, they were poorly at birth and had to be christened immediately. Your brother came in and named them.'

The woman thinks to herself; 'Oh suffering Jesus no, not me brother! He's a clueless idiot!'

Expecting the worst she asks the doctor; 'Well, what's my daughter's name?'

'Denise,' says the doctor.

The new mother is somewhat relieved.

'Wow, that's a beautiful name. I guess I was wrong about my brother. I like Denise.'

Then she asks; 'What's the boy's name?'

'Denephew,' came the reply.

172.
So two cannibals were having a chat.

One said; 'I hate my mother-in-law.'

The other one replied; 'So just eat the potatoes.'

179.

A man limped into a hospital to have his foot X-rayed, and was asked to wait for the results. Some time later an orderly appeared and handed the man a large pill.

Just then a mother with a small child in need of immediate attention entered. After the orderly disappeared with the new patient, the man hobbled over to get a glass of water, swallow the pill, and sat down to wait.

Some time later the orderly reappeared carrying a bucket of water.

'Okay,' he said. 'Let's drop the pill in this bucket and soak your foot for a while.'

180.

What men say and what it really means!

'It's a guy thing'

Translated: 'There is no rational thought pattern connected with it, and you have no chance at all of making it logical.'

'Can I help with dinner?'

Translated: 'Why the hell isn't it already on the table?'

'Uh huh,' 'Sure, honey,' or 'Yes, dear'

Translated: Absolutely nothing. It's a conditioned response.

'It would take too long to explain'

Translated: 'I have no idea how it works.'

'Take a break, honey. You're working too hard'

Translated: 'I can't hear the game over the vacuum cleaner.'

'That's interesting, dear'

Translated: 'Are you still talking?'

'You know how bad my memory is'

Translated: 'I remember the theme song to 'F Troop,' the address of the first girl I ever kissed, and the registration number of every car I've ever owned . . . but I forgot your birthday.'

'Oh, don't fuss . . . I just cut myself. It's no big deal'

Translated: 'I have actually severed a limb but will bleed to death before I admit that I'm hurt.'

'Hey, I've got my reasons for what I'm doing'

Translated: 'And I sure hope I think of some pretty soon.'

'I can't find it'

Translated: 'It didn't fall into my outstretched hands, so I'm completely clueless.'

'What did I do this time?'

Translated: 'What did you catch me at?'

'I heard you'

Translated: 'I haven't the foggiest clue what you just said and am hoping desperately that I can fake it well enough so that you don't spend the next three days yelling at me.'

'You know I could never love anyone else'

Translated: 'I am used to the way you yell at me and realise it could be worse.'

'You look terrific'

Translated: 'Oh, please don't try on one more outfit. I'm starving.'

'I'm not lost. I know exactly where we are'

Translated: 'No one will ever see us alive again.'

'We share the housework'

Translated: 'I make the messes; she cleans them up.'

:66

At the end of the tax year, the Tax Office sent an inspector to audit the books of a synagogue.

While he was checking the books he turned to the Rabbi and said; 'I notice you buy a lot of candles. What do you do with the candle drippings?'

'Good question,' noted the Rabbi. 'We save them up and send them back to the candle makers, and every now and then they send us a free box of candles.'

'Oh,' replied the auditor, somewhat disappointed that his unusual question had a practical answer.

But on he went, in his obnoxious way; 'What about all these biscuit purchases? What do you do with the crumbs?'

'Ah, yes,' replied the Rabbi, realising that the inspector was trying to trap him with an unanswerable question. 'We collect them and send them back to the manufacturer, and every now and then they send a free box of holy biscuits.'

'I see!' replied the auditor, thinking hard about how he could fluster the know-it-all Rabbi.

'Well, Rabbi,' he went on. 'What do you do with all the leftover foreskins from the circumcisions you perform?'

'Here, too, we do not waste,' answered the Rabbi.

'What we do is save up all the foreskins and send them to the Tax Office, and about once a year they send us a complete dick.'

182.

Q: What's the English version of LBW?

A: Lost, Beaten, Walloped.

183.

A large, well-established Canadian lumber camp advertised that they were looking for a good lumberjack.

The very next day, a skinny little man showed up at the camp with his axe and knocked on the head lumberjack's door. The head lumberjack took one look at the little man and told him to leave.

'Just give me a chance to show you what I can do,' said the skinny man.

'Okay, see that giant redwood over there?' said the lumberjack. 'Take your axe and go cut it down.'

The skinny man headed for the tree, and in five minutes he was back knocking on the lumberjack's door.

'I cut the tree down,' said the man.

The lumberjack couldn't believe his eyes and said; 'Where did you get the skill to chop down trees like that?'

'In the Sahara Forest,' replied the puny man.

'You mean the Sahara Desert,' said the lumberjack.

The little man laughed and answered back, 'Oh sure, that's what they call it now!'

184.
A young Aussie lad moved to London and went to Harrods looking for a job.

The manager asked; 'Do you have any sales experience?'

The young man answered; 'Yeah, I was a salesman back home.'

The manager liked the Aussie so he gave him the job. His first day on the job was challenging and busy, but he got through it.

After the store was locked up, the manager came down and asked; 'OK, so how many sales did you make today?'

The Aussie said; 'One.' The manager groaned and continued; 'Just one? Our sales people average 20 or 30 sales a day. How much was the sale for?'

'124,237 pounds'

The manager choked and exclaimed, '124,237!!! What the hell did you sell him?'

'Well, first I sold him a small fish hook, then a medium fish hook, and then I sold him a new fishing rod. Then I asked him where he was going fishing and he said down at the coast, so I told him he would need a boat, so we went down to the boat department and I sold him that twin-engined Power Cat.

'Then he said he didn't think his Honda Civic would pull it, so I took him down to car sales and I sold him the 4x4 Suzuki.'

The manager, incredulous, said; 'You mean to tell me a guy came in here to buy a fish hook and you sold him a boat and 4x4?'

'No, no, no. He came in here to buy a box of tampons for his lady friend and I said . . . "Well, since your weekend's buggered, you might as well go fishing."'

4TH OF JULY

Bush's tragedy

One day, President Bush visited an elementary school. All the kids were so excited to get to meet the President. He began to talk to them and asked them to define the word 'tragedy'.

'Well,' one girl replied, 'If my mummy ran over my dog, Rover, that would be a tragedy!'

The President smiled at the little girl and said, 'No, sweetie. That would be an accident! Can anyone give it a try?'

A little boy sitting across the room raised his hand and said, 'I know! I know! If our bus driver ran off of a cliff and killed everyone!'

The President shook his head and said, 'No son. That would be a great loss! Doesn't anyone know of a good example of a tragedy?'

A small girl raised her hand and said, 'Well, Mr. President, if you and Laura were in Air Force One and it was hit by a missile and blown to smithereens, most people would think that that was a tragedy!'

'Very good,' he said. 'And what was your reason for that answer?'

'Well,' she said, 'It would not be an accident and it sure would not be a great loss!'

186.
At 75 years old, George went for his annual physical. All of his tests came back with normal results.

Dr Smith said; 'George, everything looks great physically. How are you doing mentally and emotionally? Are you at peace with yourself, and do you have a good relationship with God?'

George replied; 'Yeah, God and me are tight. He knows that I have poor eyesight, so he's fixed it so that when I get up in the middle of the night to go to the bathroom (poof) the light goes on, and when I'm done (poof) the light goes off.'

'Wow!' commented Dr Smith. 'That's incredible!'

A little later in the day Dr Smith called George's wife.

'Ethel,' he said. 'George is doing fine. Physically he's great. But, I had to call because I'm in awe of his relationship with God. Is it true that he gets up during the night and (poof) the light goes on in the bathroom, and then when he is through (poof) the light goes off?'

Ethel exclaimed, 'Oh, my God, he's peeing in the refrigerator again!'

187.
In a crowded city at a busy bus stop, a beautiful young blonde woman wearing a tight leather skirt was waiting for a bus. As the bus stopped and it was her turn to get on, she became aware that her skirt was too tight to allow her leg to come up to the height of the first step of the bus.

Slightly embarrassed and with a quick smile to the bus driver, she reached behind her to unzip her skirt a little, thinking that this would give her enough slack to raise her leg. She tried to take the step, only to discover that she couldn't.

So, a little more embarrassed, she once again reached behind her to unzip her skirt a little more and, for the second time, attempted the step. Once again, much to her chagrin, she could not raise her leg.

With a little smile to the driver, she again reached behind to unzip a little more and again was unable to take the step.

About this time, a large bloke who was standing behind her picked her up easily by the waist and placed her gently on the step of the bus.

She went ballistic and turned to the would-be Samaritan and screeched; 'How dare you touch my body! I don't even know you!'

The bloke smiled and said; 'Well, ma'am, normally I would agree with you, but after you unzipped my fly three times, I kinda figured we was friends.'

188.

A guy goes to the supermarket and notices an attractive woman waving at him. She says; 'Hello.'

He's rather taken aback because he can't place where he knows her from. So he says; 'Do you know me?'

To which she replies; 'I think you're the father of one of my kids.'

Now his mind travels back to the only time he has ever been unfaithful to his wife and says; 'My God, are you the stripper from my bachelor party that I made love to on the pool table with all my buddies watching while your partner whipped my butt with wet celery?'

She looks into his eyes and says calmly; 'No. I'm your son's teacher.'

One morning the husband returns to the lakeside after several hours of fishing and decides to take a nap. Although not familiar with the lake, the wife decides to take the boat out on her own.

She motors out a short distance, anchors, and reads her book.

Along comes a Ranger in his boat. He pulls up alongside the woman and says; 'Good morning, Ma'am. What are you doing?'

'Reading a book,' she replies (thinking, Isn't that bleeding obvious?).

'You're in a Restricted Fishing Area,' he informs her.

'I'm sorry, officer, but I'm not fishing. I'm reading.'

'Yes, but you have all the equipment. For all I know you could start at any moment. I'll have to take you in and write you up a fine ticket.'

'If you do that, I'll have to charge you with sexual assault,' says the woman.

'But I haven't even touched you,' says the Ranger.

'That's true, but you have all the equipment. For all I know you could start at any moment.'

A man and a woman were sitting beside each other in the first class section of an airplane. The woman sneezed, took out a tissue, gently wiped her nose, then visibly shuddered for ten to 15 seconds.

The man went back to his reading. A few minutes later, the woman sneezed again, took a tissue, wiped her nose, then shuddered violently once more. Assuming that the woman might have a cold, the man was still curious about the shuddering. A few more minutes passed when the woman sneezed yet again.

As before she took a tissue, wiped her nose, her body shaking ever more than before. Unable to restrain his curiosity, the man turned to the woman and said; 'I couldn't help but notice that you've sneezed three times, wiped your nose and then shuddered violently. Are you ok?'

'I am sorry if I disturbed you, I have a very rare medical condition. Whenever I sneeze I have an orgasm.'

The man, more than a bit embarrassed, was still curious. 'I have never heard of that condition before,' he said. 'Are you taking anything for it?'

The woman nodded; 'Pepper.'

191.

Two blonde girls were working for the city public works department.

 One would dig a hole and the other would follow behind her and fill the hole in. They worked up one side of the street, then down the other, then moved on to the next street, working furiously all day without rest.

One girl digging a hole, the other girl filling it in again.

An onlooker was amazed at their hard work, but couldn't understand what they were doing.

So he asked the hole digger; 'I'm impressed by the effort you two are putting into your work, but I don't get it-why do you dig a hole, only to have your partner follow behind and fill it up again?'

The hole digger wiped her brow and sighed; 'Well, I suppose it probably looks odd because we're normally a three-person team. But today the girl who plants the trees called in sick.'

192.

Q: What is the most proficient form of footwork displayed by English batsmen?

A: The walk back to the pavilion.

193.

A woman went to a discount store's service counter and told the clerk she wanted a refund for the toaster she bought because it wouldn't work. The clerk told her that he can't give her a refund because she bought it on special.

Suddenly, the woman threw her arms up in the air and started screaming; 'Pinch my nipples, pinch my nipples, pinch my nipples!'

The befuddled clerk ran away to get the store manager in front of a growing crowd of customers.

The manager comes to the woman and asks; 'Ma'am what's wrong?'

She explained the problem with the toaster, and he also told her that he can't give her a refund because she bought it on special.

Once again, the woman throws her arms up in the air and screamed; 'Pinch my nipples, pinch my nipples, pinch my nipples!'

A huge crowd now gathered around the discussion.

In shock, the store manager pleads; 'Ma'am, why are you saying that?'

In a huff, the woman says; 'Because, I like to have my nipples pinched when I'm being screwed!!'

The crowd broke into applause and the woman's money was promptly refunded.

194.

Fresh from a shower, a woman stands in front of the mirror, complaining to her husband that her breasts are too small.

Instead of automatically telling her it's not so, the husband uncharacteristically comes up with a suggestion; 'If you want your breasts to grow, then every day take a piece of toilet paper and rub it between your breasts for a few seconds.'

Willing to try anything, the woman grabs a piece of toilet paper and stands in front of the mirror, rubbing it between her breasts.

'How long will this take?' she asks.

'They will grow larger over a period of years,' he replies.

'Do you really think rubbing a piece of toilet paper between my breasts every day will make my breasts larger over the years?' she quips.

Without missing a beat he says; 'Worked for your bum, didn't it?'

He's still alive, and with a great deal of physio, he may even walk again. Stupid, stupid man.

195.

One night, as a couple lays down for bed, the husband starts rubbing his wife's arm romantically.

The wife turns over and says; 'I'm sorry honey, I've got a gynaecologist appointment tomorrow and I want to stay fresh.'

The husband, rejected, turns over. A few minutes later, he rolls back over and taps his wife again.

'Do you have a dentist appointment tomorrow too?'

196.

Bill worked in a pickle factory. He had been employed there for a number of years when he came home one day to confess to his wife that he had a terrible compulsion.

He had an urge to stick his penis into the pickle slicer.

His wife suggested that he should see a sex therapist to talk about it, but Bill said he would be too embarrassed. He vowed to overcome the compulsion on his own.

One day a few weeks later, Bill came home and his wife could see at once that something was seriously wrong.

'What's wrong, Bill?' she asked.

'Do you remember that I told you how I had this tremendous urge to put my penis into the pickle slicer?' he explained.

'Oh, Bill, you didn't,' she exclaimed.

'Yes, I did,' he replied.

'My God, Bill, what happened?'

'I got fired.'

'No, Bill. I mean, what happened with the pickle slicer?'

'Oh . . . she got fired too.'

197.

A blonde went to an eye doctor to have her eyes checked for glasses. The doctor directed her to read various letters with the left eye while covering the right eye.

The blonde was so mixed up about which eye was which that the eye doctor, in disgust, took a paper lunch bag with a hole to see through, covered up the appropriate eye and asked her to read the letters.

As he did so, he noticed the blonde had tears streaming down her face.

'Look,' said the doctor, 'there's no need to get emotional about getting glasses.'

'I know,' agreed the blonde, 'But I kind of had my heart set on wire frames.'

198.

His name was Fleming, and he was a poor Scottish farmer. One day, while trying to make a living for his family, he heard a cry for help coming from a nearby bog. He dropped his tools and ran to the bog.

There, mired to his waist in black muck, was a terrified boy, screaming and struggling to free himself. Farmer Fleming saved the lad from what could have been a slow and terrifying death.

The next day, a fancy carriage pulled up to the Scotsman's sparse surroundings An elegantly dressed nobleman stepped out and introduced himself as the father of the boy Farmer Fleming had saved.

'I want to repay you,' said the nobleman. 'You saved my son's life.'

'No, I can't accept payment for what I did,' the Scottish farmer replied waving off the offer. At that moment, the farmer's own son came to the door of the family hovel.

'Is that your son?' the nobleman asked.

'Yes,' the farmer replied proudly.

'I'll make you a deal. Let me provide him with the level of education my own son will enjoy. If the lad is anything like his father, he'll no doubt grow to be a man we both will be proud of.' And that he did.

Farmer Fleming's son attended the very best schools and in time, graduated from St Mary's Hospital Medical School in London, and went on to become known throughout the world as the noted Sir Alexander Fleming, the discoverer of Penicillin.

Years afterward, the same nobleman's son who was saved from the bog was stricken with pneumonia.

What saved his life this time? Penicillin.

The name of the nobleman? Lord Randolph Churchill.

His son's name? Sir Winston Churchill.

Someone once said: What goes around comes around.

199.

A man escaped from prison by digging a tunnel from his cell to the outside world.

Emerging in the middle of a pre-school playground, he shouted; 'I'm free . . . I'm free!!!'

'So what?' said a little girl. 'I'm four.'

200.

A guy walked into a barber shop and asked; 'How long before I can get a haircut?'

The barber looked around the shop full of customers and said; 'About three hours.' The guy left.

A few days later the same guy came back and asked; 'How long before I can get a haircut?'

The barber looked around the shop and said; 'About two hours.' The guy left.

A week later the same guy came back yet again and asked; 'How long before I can get a haircut?'

The barber looked around the shop and said; 'About half an hour.' The guy left in a hurry!

The barber then turned to a friend and said; 'Hey Bill, do me a favour. Follow that guy and see where he goes. He keeps asking how long he has to wait for a haircut, but then he doesn't come back.'

A little while later, Bill returned to the shop looking like he'd just seen a ghost.

'So where does that guy go when he leaves?' asked the barber.

Bill hesitated then said; 'Your house!'

201.
Two Scots, Archie and Jock, are sitting in the pub discussing Jock's forthcoming wedding.

'Ach, it's all going grand,' says Jock. 'I've got everything organised already: the flowers, the church, the cars, the reception, the rings, the minister, even ma stag night.'

Archie nods approvingly.

'Heavens, I've even bought a kilt to be married in!' continues Jock.

'A kilt?' exclaims Archie. 'That's braw, you'll look pure smart in that!'

'And what's the tartan?' Archie then enquires.

'Och,' says Jock. 'I'd imagine she'll be in white . . .'

Wiremu, a New Zealander, was in Australia to watch the upcoming Bledisloe Cup and was not feeling well, so he decided to see a doctor.

'Hey doc, I dun't feel so good, ey,' said Wiremu.

The doctor gave him a thorough examination and informed Wiremu that he had long existing and advanced prostate problems and that the only cure was testicular removal.

'No way doc,' replied Wiremu. 'I'm gitting a sicond opinion, ey!'

The second Aussie doctor gave Wiremu the same diagnosis and also advised him that testicular removal was the only cure.

Not surprisingly, Wiremu refused the treatment.

Wiremu was devastated but, with the Bledisloe Cup just around the corner, he found an expat Kiwi doctor and decided to get one last opinion from someone he could trust.

The Kiwi doctor examined him and said; 'Wiremu Cuzzy Bro, you huv da prostate suckness dar, ey.'

'What's the cure thin doc?' asked Wiremu hoping for a different answer.

'Wull, Wiremu', said the Kiwi doctor. 'Wi're gonna huv to cut off your balls there bro.'

'Phew, thunk god for thut!' said Wiremu. 'Those Aussie b.a.s.t.a.r.d.s wanted to take my test tickets off me!'

203.

Two guys chatting in a pub; 'I didn't sleep with my wife before marriage, did you?'

'Don't know, mate. What's her name?'

204.

Little boy goes to father; 'Dad, where did my intelligence come from?'

Father replies; 'Must be from your mother, I've still got mine.'

205.

When the store manager returned from lunch, he noticed his clerk's hand was bandaged, but before he could ask about the bandage, the clerk had some very good news for him.

'Guess what, sir?' the clerk said. 'I finally sold that terrible, ugly suit we've had so long!'

'Do you mean that repulsive pink-and-blue double-breasted thing?' the manager asked.

'That's the one!'

'That's great!' the manager cried, 'I thought we'd never get rid of that monstrosity! That had to be the ugliest suit we've ever had! But tell me, why is your hand bandaged?'

'Oh,' the clerk replied, 'after I sold the guy that suit, his seeing-eye dog bit me.'

206.

A teacher is explaining biology to her 4th grade students.

'Human beings are the only animals that stutter,' she says.

A little girl raises her hand.

'I had a kitty-cat who stuttered,' she volunteered.

The teacher, knowing how precious some of these stories could become, asked the girl to describe the incident.

'Well,' she began. 'I was in the back yard with my kitty and the Rottweiler who lives next door got a running start and before we knew it, he jumped over the fence into our yard!'

'That must've been scary,' said the teacher.

'It sure was,' said the little girl.

'My kitty went "Fffff, Fffff, Fffff" . . . and before he could say "F@#k," the Rottweiler ate him!'

207.

A man goes to see the Rabbi.

'Rabbi, something terrible is happening and I have to talk to you about it.'

The Rabbi asked; 'What's wrong?'

The man replied; 'My wife is poisoning me.'

The Rabbi, very surprised by this, asks; 'How can that be?'

The man then pleads; 'I'm telling you, I'm certain she's poisoning me. What should I do?'

The Rabbi then offers; 'Tell you what. I should talk to her. Let me talk to her. I'll see what I can find out and I'll let you know.'

A week later the Rabbi calls the man and says; 'I spoke to your wife. Spoke to her on the phone for three hours. For three hours I spoke to her! You want I should give you my advice?'

The man said, 'Yes,' and the Rabbi replied; 'Take the poison!'

208.

On their wedding night, the young bride approached her new husband and asked for $20 for their first lovemaking encounter. In his highly aroused state, her husband readily agreed.

This scenario was repeated each time they made love, for more than 30 years, with him thinking that it was a cute way for her to afford new clothes and other incidentals that she needed.

Arriving home around noon one day, she was surprised to find her husband at home.

During the next few minutes, he explained that his employer was going through a process of corporate downsizing, and he had been let go.

It was unlikely that, at the age of 59, he'd be able to find another position that paid anywhere near what he'd been earning and, therefore, they were financially ruined.

Calmly, his wife handed him a bank book which showed more than 30 years of steady deposits and interest totalling nearly $1 million.

Then she showed him certificates of deposits issued by the bank which were worth over $2 million, and informed him that they were one of the largest depositors in the bank.

She explained that for the more than three decades she had charged him for sex and these holdings had multiplied and these were the results of her savings and investments.

Faced with evidence of cash and investments worth over $3 million, her husband was so astounded he could barely speak.

But finally he found his voice and blurted out; 'If I'd had any idea what you were doing, I would have given you all my business!'

That's when she shot him.

You know, sometimes, men just don't know when to keep their mouths shut.

209.

Doctor examines wife and says to husband; 'I don't like the look of your wife.'

'Me neither,' says the husband. 'But she's a great cook and good with the kids.'

210.

A man enters a bar and orders a drink. The bar has a robot bartender.

The robot serves him a perfectly prepared cocktail, and then asks him; 'What's your IQ?'

The man replies; '150.'

The robot proceeds to make conversation about global warming, quantum physics and spirituality, bio-mimicry, environmental interconnectedness, string theory, nano-technology, and sexual proclivities.

The customer is very impressed and thinks; 'This is really cool.'

He decides to test the robot. He walks out of the bar, turns around, and comes back in for another drink. Again, the robot serves him the perfectly prepared drink and asks him; 'What's your IQ?'

The man responds; 'About a 100.'

Immediately the robot starts talking, but this time, about football, Bathurst 1000, cricket, supermodels, favourite fast foods, guns, and women's breasts.

Really impressed, the man leaves the bar and decides to give the robot one more test.

He heads out and returns, the robot serves him and asks; 'What's your IQ?'

The man replies; 'Er, 50, I reckon.'

And the robot says . . . realllllllly slowwwwwwly; 'So ya gonna follow the All Blacks again this year?'

211. A cat died and went to Heaven. God met her at the gates and said; 'You have been a good cat all these years. Anything you want is yours for the asking.'

The cat thought for a minute and then said; 'All my life I lived on a farm and slept on hard wooden floors. I would like a real fluffy pillow to sleep on.'

God said; 'Say no more.'

Instantly the cat had a huge fluffy pillow.

A few days later, six mice were killed in an accident and they all went to Heaven together. God met the mice at the gates with the same offer that He made to the cat.

The mice said; 'Well, we have had to run all of our lives from cats, dogs, and even people with brooms! If we could just have some little roller skates, we would not have to run again.'

God answered; 'It is done.'

All the mice had beautiful little roller skates.

About a week later, God decided to check on the cat. He found her sound asleep on her fluffy pillow.

God gently awakened the cat and asked; 'Is everything okay? How have you been doing? Are you happy?'

The cat replied; 'Oh, it is WONDERFUL. I have never been so happy in my life. The pillow is so fluffy, and those little Meals on Wheels you have been sending over are delicious!'

212.

One day, a seamstress was sewing while sitting close to a river and her thimble fell into the river.

When she cried out, the Lord appeared and asked; 'My dear child, why are you crying?'

The seamstress replied that her thimble had fallen into the water and that she needed it to help her husband in making a living for their family.

The Lord dipped his hand into the water and pulled up a golden thimble set with pearls.

'Is this your thimble?' the Lord asked.

The seamstress replied; 'No.'

The Lord again dipped into the river. He held out a silver thimble ringed with sapphires.

'Is this your thimble?' the Lord asked again.

The seamstress replied; 'No'

The Lord reached down again and came up with a leather thimble.

'Is this your thimble?' the Lord asked.

The seamstress replied; 'Yes.'

The Lord was pleased with the woman's honesty and gave her all three thimbles to keep and the seamstress went home happy.

Some years later, the seamstress was walking with her husband along the same riverbank and her husband fell into the river and disappeared under the water.

When she cried out, the Lord again appeared and asked her; 'Why are you crying?'

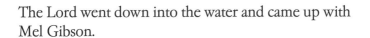

'Oh Lord, my husband has fallen into the river!'

The Lord went down into the water and came up with Mel Gibson.

'Is this your husband?' the Lord asked.

'YES,' cried the seamstress.

The Lord was furious. 'YOU LIED! That is an untruth!

The seamstress replied; 'Oh, forgive me, my Lord. It is a misunderstanding. You see, if I had said 'No' to Mel Gibson, you would have come up with Tom Cruise. Then, if I said 'No' to him, you would have come up with my husband and had I then said 'Yes' you would have given me all three. Lord, I'm not in the best of health and would not be able to take care of all three husbands, so that's why I said 'Yes' to Mel Gibson.'

The moral of this story is: Whenever a woman lies, it's for a good and honourable reason and in the best interest of others. That's our story, and we're sticking to it!

213.

Q: 'Mummy, Mummy, why is Dad running in zig zags?'

A: 'Shut up and keep shooting.'

214.

A blonde lady motorist was about two hours from Melbourne when she was flagged down by a man whose truck had broken down.

The man walked up to the car and asked; 'Are you going to Melbourne?'

'Sure,' answered the blonde. 'Do you need a lift?'

'Not for me. I'll be spending the next three hours fixing my truck. My problem is I've got two chimpanzees in the back of the truck which have to be taken to the Melbourne Zoo. They're a bit stressed already so I don't want to keep them on the road all day. Could you possibly take them to the zoo for me? I'll give you $100 for your trouble.'

'I'd be happy to,' said the blonde.

So the two chimpanzees were ushered into the back seat of the blonde's car and carefully strapped into their seat belts. Off they went.

Five hours later, the truck driver was driving through the heart of Melbourne when suddenly he was horrified! There was the blonde walking down the street and holding hands with the two chimps, much to the amusement of a big crowd.

With a screech of brakes he pulled off the road and ran over to the blonde.

'What the heck are you doing here?' he demanded. 'I gave you $100 to take these chimpanzees to the zoo.'

'Yes, I know you did,' said the blonde. 'But we had money left over so now we're going to the Aquarium.'

215.

A little old lady, well into her 80s, slowly enters the front door of a sex shop. Obviously very unstable on her feet, she wobbles the few feet across the store to the counter.

Finally arriving at the counter and grabbing it for support, stuttering she asks the sales clerk; 'Dddooo youuuu hhhave dddddiillllldosss?'

The clerk, politely trying not to burst out laughing, replies; 'Yes we do have dildos. Actually we carry many different models.'

The old woman then asks; 'Ddddoooo yyyouuuu ccaarrryy aaa pppinkk onnee, tttenn inchessss lllong aaandd aabbboutt ttwoo inchesss ththiickk . . . aaand rrunns by bbaatteries ?'

The clerk responds; 'Yes we do.'

'Ddddooo yyoooouuuu kknnnoooww hhhowww tttooo ttturrrnnn ttthe ssunoooffabbitch offfff?'

216.

'Sixty is the worst age to be,' said the 60-year-old man. 'You always feel like you have to pee and most of the time you stand there and nothing comes out.'

'Ah, that's nothing,' said the 70-year-old. 'When you're seventy, you don't have a bowel movement any more. You take laxatives, eat bran, sit on the toilet all day and nothing comes out!'

'Actually,' said the 80-year-old. 'Eighty is the worst age of all.'

'Do you have trouble peeing, too?' asked the 60-year old.

'No, I pee every morning at 6 am. I pee like a racehorse on a flat rock, no problem at all.'

'So, do you have a problem with your bowel movement?'

'No, I have one every morning at 6:30.'

Exasperated, the 60-year-old said; 'You pee every morning at 6:00 and crap every morning at 6:30. So what's so bad about being 80?'

'I don't wake up until 7.'

217.

A skinny little white guy goes into an elevator, looks up and sees this HUGE black guy standing next to him.

The big guy sees the little guy staring at him, looks down and says; '7 feet tall, 350 pounds, 20 inch dick, 3 pound left testicle, 3 pound right testicle, Turner Brown.'

The little white man faints and falls to the floor.

The big guy kneels down and shakes him to bring him round.

The big guy says; 'What's wrong with you?'

In a weak voice the little guy says; 'What EXACTLY did you say to me?'

The big dude says; 'I saw your curious look and figured I'd just give you the answers to the questions everyone always asks me. I'm 7 feet tall, I weigh 350 pounds, I have a 20 inch dick, my left testicle weighs 3 pounds, my right testicle weighs 3 pounds, and my name is Turner Brown.'

The small guy says, 'Turner Brown? Oh sweet Jesus, I thought you said 'Turn around!'

218.

A father passing by his son's bedroom, was astonished to see the bed was nicely made, and everything was cleaned up.

Then he saw an envelope, propped up prominently on the pillow. It was addressed; 'Dad.'

With the worst premonition, he opened the envelope and read the letter, with trembling hands.

Dear, Dad. It is with great regret and sorrow that I'm writing you. I had to elope with my new girlfriend, because I wanted to avoid a scene with Mum and you.

I've been finding real passion with Stacy and she is so nice, but I knew you would not approve of her because of all her piercings, tattoos, her tight motorcycle clothes, and because she is so much older than I am.

But it's not only the passion, Dad. She's pregnant. Stacy said that we will be very happy. She owns a trailer in the woods, and has a stack of firewood for the whole winter. We share a dream of having many more children.

Stacy has opened my eyes to the fact that marijuana doesn't really hurt anyone. We'll be growing it for ourselves, and trading it with the other people in the commune, for all the cocaine and ecstasy we want.

In the meantime, we'll pray that science will find a cure for AIDS, so Stacy can get better. She sure deserves it!

Don't worry Dad, I'm 15, and I know how to take care of myself. Someday, I'm sure we'll be back to visit, so you can get to know your many grandchildren.

Love,

Your son, John

P.S. Dad, none of the above is true. I'm over at Tommy's house. I just wanted to remind you that there are worse things in life than the school report that's on my desk. I love you! Call when it is safe for me to come home.

219.

Judge reviewing a case very carefully; 'I've decided to give your wife $700 a week.'

Husband says; 'That's fair. I will try and give her a few bucks myself.'

220.

In the dead of summer a fly was resting on a leaf beside a lake.

The hot, dry fly that said to no one in particular; 'Gosh. If I move down three inches, I will feel the mist from the water and I will be refreshed.'

There was a fish in the water thinking; 'Gosh. If that fly moves down three inches, I can eat him.'

There was a bear on the shore thinking; 'Gosh. If that fly moves down three inches that fish will jump for the fly and I will grab him.'

It also happened that a hunter was farther up the bank of the lake preparing to eat a cheese sandwich. 'Gosh,' he thought. 'If that fly moves down three inches and that fish leaps for it, that bear will expose himself and grab for the fish. I'll shoot the bear and have a proper lunch.'

You probably think this is enough activity on one bank of a lake, but I can tell you there's more.

A wee mouse by the hunter's foot was thinking; 'Gosh. If that fly moves down three inches and that fish jumps for that fly and that bear grabs for that fish the dumb hunter will shoot the bear and drop his cheese sandwich.'

A cat lurking in the bushes took in this scene and thought; 'Gosh. If that fly moves down three inches and that fish jumps for that fly and that bear grabs for that fish and that hunter shoots that bear and that mouse makes off with the cheese sandwich then I can have mouse for lunch.'

The poor fly is finally so hot and so dry that he heads down for the cooling mist of the water. The fish swallows the fly. The bear grabs the fish. The hunter shoots the bear. The mouse grabs the cheese sandwich. The cat jumps for the mouse. The mouse ducks. The cat falls into the water and drowns.

And the moral of the story is: Whenever a fly goes down three inches, some pussy is in serious danger.

221. **Q:** Why is it dangerous do maths in a jungle?

A: 'Cause if you add four and four you get ate.

222.

The wife comes home early and finds her husband in their master bedroom making love to a beautiful, sexy young lady!

'You unfaithful, disrespectful pig! What are you doing? How dare you do this to me, the faithful wife, the mother of your children! I'm leaving this house; I want a divorce!'

The husband replies; 'Wait. Wait a minute! Before you leave, at least listen to what happened.'

'Hmmmmmm, I don't know,' said the wife. 'Well, it'll be the last thing I will hear from you. But make it fast, you unfaithful pig!'

The husband begins to tell his story; 'While driving home this young lady asks for a ride. I saw her so defenceless that I went ahead and allowed her in my car. I noticed that she was very thin, not well-dressed, and very dirty. She mentioned that she had not eaten for three days.

'With great compassion and hurt, I brought her home and warmed up the enchiladas that I made for you last night, the ones you wouldn't eat because you're afraid you'll gain weight.

'The poor thing practically devours them. Since she was very dirty I asked her to take a shower. While she was showering, I noticed her clothes were dirty and full of holes, so I threw them away. Since she needed clothes, I gave her the pair of jeans that you have had for a few years, and that you can no longer wear because they are too tight on you.

'I also gave her the blouse that I gave you on our anniversary, the one you don't wear because I don't have good taste. I gave her the pullover that my sister gave you for Christmas, the one you refuse to wear just to bother my sister; and I also gave her the boots that you bought at the expensive boutique that you never wore again after you saw your co-worker wearing the same pair.'

The husband continues his story; 'The young woman was very grateful to me and I walked her to the door, at which point she turned around, and with tears coming out of her eyes, she asks me: "Sir, do you have anything else that your wife does not use?"'

223.

'I believe that sex is one of the most beautiful, natural, wholesome things that money can buy.'

Tom Clancy

224.

'You know "that look" women get when they want sex? Me neither.'

Steve Martin

225.

'Having sex is like playing bridge. If you don't have a good partner, you'd better have a good hand.'

Woody Allen

226.

'Bisexuality immediately doubles your chances for a date on Saturday night.'

Rodney Dangerfield

227.

'There are a number of mechanical devices which increase sexual arousal, particularly in women. Chief among these is the Mercedes-Benz 500SL.'

Lynn Lavner

228.

'Sex is one of the nine reasons for reincarnation. The other eight are unimportant.'

George Burns

229.

'Women might be able to fake orgasms. But men can fake whole relationships.'

Sharon Stone

230.   **LABOUR DAY**

Work like you don't need the money
Love like you've never been hurt
Dance like nobody's watching
Sing like nobody's listening
Live like it's Heaven on Earth

231.

'My girlfriend always laughs during sex . . . no matter what she's reading.'

Steve Jobs

232.

'My mother never saw the irony in calling me a son-of-a-bitch.'

Jack Nicholson

233.

'Women need a reason to have sex. Men just need a place.'

Billy Crystal

234.

'According to a new survey, women say they feel more comfortable undressing in front of men than they do undressing in front of other women. They say that women are too judgmental, where, of course, men are just grateful.'

Robert De Niro

235.

Three men are sitting in the maternity ward of a hospital waiting for the imminent birth of their respective children.

One is an Australian, one a New Zealander and the other a West Indian. They are all very nervous and pacing the floor . . . as you do in these situations.

All of a sudden the doctor bursts through the double doors saying; 'Gentlemen you won't believe this but your wives have all had their babies within five minutes of each other.'

The men are beside themselves with happiness and joy.

'And,' said the doctor, 'they have all had little boys.'

The fathers are ecstatic and congratulate each other over and over.

'However we do have one slight problem,' the doctor said. 'In all the confusion we may have mixed the babies up getting them to the nursery and we would be grateful if you could join us there to try and help identify them.'

With that the Aussie raced passed the doctor and bolted to the nursery. Once inside he picked up a dark skinned infant with dreadlocks saying; 'There's no doubt about it, this boy is mine!'

The doctor looked bewildered and said; 'Well sir of all the babies I would have thought that maybe this child could be of West Indian descent.'

'That's a maybe so,' said the Aussie. 'But one of the other two is a Kiwi and I'm not taking the risk.'

236.

A young pretty girl worked in a local bakery shop and was required to wear quite a short skirt as part of the uniform. The problem was, the shop was quite small and the bread was stacked on high shelves so a ladder had to be used to get certain products.

One of these was raisin bread.

On the days when raisin bread was on special the queues were four deep and there was a noticeable increase in customers, particularly elderly gentlemen.

One day she'd been up and down the ladder constantly and by four o'clock she was exhausted.

Turning to her next customer, a very wrinkled old man who had been waiting in the queue for quite a while she sharply said; 'And, I suppose yours is raisin?'

'No', he replied. 'But there's a little quiver there.'

231.

An elderly couple visits McDonalds. He ordered one hamburger, one order of French fries and one drink.

The old man unwrapped the plain hamburger and carefully cut it in half. He placed one half in front of his wife. He then carefully counted out the French fries, dividing them into two piles, and neatly placed one pile in front of his wife.

He took a sip of the drink, his wife took a sip and then set the cup down between them.

As he began to eat his few bites of hamburger, the people around them kept looking over and whispering.

You could tell they were thinking; 'That poor old couple. All they can afford is one meal for the two of them.'

As the man began to eat his fries a young man came to the table. He politely offered to buy another meal for the old couple.

The old man said they were just fine. They were used to sharing everything.

The surrounding people noticed the little old lady hadn't eaten a bite. She sat there watching her husband eat and occasionally taking turns sipping the drink.

Again, the young man came over and begged them to let him buy another meal for them. This time the old woman said; 'No thank you, we are used to sharing everything.'

As the old man finished and was wiping his face neatly with the napkin, the young man again came over to the little old lady who had yet to eat a single bite of food and asked; 'What is it you are waiting for?'

She answered; 'The TEETH!'

238.

In the year 2007, the Lord came unto Noah, who was now living in England and said; 'Once again, the earth has become wicked and over-populated, and I see the end of all flesh before me. Build another Ark and save two of every living thing along with a few good humans.'

He gave Noah the CAD drawings, saying; 'You have six months to build the Ark before I start the unending rain for 40 days and 40 nights.'

Six months later, the Lord looked down and saw Noah weeping in his yard . . . but no Ark.

'Noah!' He roared. 'I'm about to start the rain! Where is the Ark?'

'Forgive me, Lord,' begged Noah. 'But things have changed. I needed a Building Regulations Approval. I've been arguing with the Fire Brigade about the need for a sprinkler system. My neighbours claim that I should have obtained planning permission for building the Ark in my garden because it is a development of the site even though in my view it is a temporary structure. We had to go to appeal for a decision.

'Then the Department of Transport demanded a bond be posted for the future costs of moving power lines and other overhead obstructions, to clear the passage for the Ark's move to the sea. I told them that the sea would be coming to us, but they would hear nothing of it.

'Getting the wood was another problem. All the decent trees have Tree Preservation Orders on them and we live in a Site of Special Scientific Interest set up in order to protect the spotted owl. I tried to convince the environmentalists that I needed the wood to save the owls . . . but no go!

'When I started gathering the animals, the RSPCA sued me. They insisted that I was confining wild animals against their will. They argued the accommodation was too restrictive, and it was cruel and inhumane to put so many animals in a confined space.

'Then the County Council, the Environment Agency and the Rivers Authority ruled that I couldn't build the Ark until they'd conducted an environmental impact study on your proposed flood.

'I'm still trying to resolve a complaint with the Equal Opportunities Commission on how many minorities I'm supposed to hire for my building team.

'The trades unions say I can't use my sons. They insist I have to hire only accredited workers with Ark-building experience.

'To make matters worse, Customs and Excise seized all my assets, claiming I'm trying to leave the country illegally with endangered species.

'So, forgive me, Lord, but it would take at least ten years for me to finish this Ark.'

Suddenly the skies cleared, the sun began to shine, and a rainbow stretched across the sky. Noah looked up in wonder and asked; 'You mean you're not going to destroy the world?'

'No,' said the Lord. 'The government beat me to it.'

239.

The pastor entered his donkey in a race and it won.

The pastor was so pleased with the donkey that he entered it in the race again, and it won again.

The local paper read: PASTOR'S ASS OUT FRONT.

The Bishop was so upset with this kind of publicity that he ordered the pastor not to enter the donkey in another race.

The next day, the local paper headline read: BISHOP SCRATCHES PASTOR'S ASS.

This was too much for the Bishop, so he ordered the pastor to get rid of the donkey.

The pastor decided to give it to a nun in a nearby convent. The local paper, hearing of the news, posted the following headline the next day: NUN HAS BEST ASS IN TOWN.

The Bishop fainted. He informed the nun that she would have to get rid of the donkey, so she sold it to a farmer for $10.

The next day the paper read: NUN SELLS ASS FOR $10.

This was too much for the Bishop, so he ordered the nun to buy back the donkey and lead it to the plains where it could run wild.

The next day the headlines read: NUN ANNOUNCES HER ASS IS WILD AND FREE.

The Bishop was buried the next day.

The moral of the story is: Being concerned about public opinion can bring you much grief and misery and even shorten your life. So be yourself and enjoy life. Stop worrying about everyone else's ass and you'll be a lot happier and live longer!

240.

A pirate walked into a bar and the bartender said; 'Hey, I haven't seen you in a while. What happened? You look terrible.'

'What do you mean?' said the pirate. 'I feel fine.'

'What about the wooden leg? You didn't have that before.'

'Well, we were in a battle and I got hit with a canon ball, but I'm fine now.'

'Well, OK, but what about that hook? What happened to your hand?'

'We were in another battle. I boarded a ship and got into a sword fight. My hand was cut off. I got fitted with a hook. I'm fine, really.'

'What about that eye patch?'

'Oh, one day we were at sea and a flock of birds flew over. I looked up and one of them pooped in my eye.'

'You're kidding,' said the bartender. 'But surely you couldn't lose an eye just from a little bird poop?'

'It was my first day with the hook.'

241.
A distinguished young woman on a flight from Switzerland asked the priest beside her; 'Father, may I ask a favour?'

'Of course. What may I do for you?' said the priest

'Well, I bought an expensive electronic hairdryer that is well over the Customs limits, and I'm afraid they'll confiscate it. Is there anyway you could carry it through Customs for me? Under your robes perhaps?'

'I would love to help you, dear, but I must warn you: I will not lie.'

'With your honest face, Father, no one will question you.'

When they got to Customs, she let the priest go ahead of her.

The official asked; 'Father, do you have anything to declare?'

'From the top of my head down to my waist, I have nothing to declare.'

The official thought this answer strange, so asked; 'And what do you have to declare from your waist to the floor?'

'I have a marvellous little instrument designed to be used on a woman, but which is, to date, unused.'

Roaring with laughter, the official said; 'Go ahead, Father.'

'Next!'

242.
The teacher gave her fifth grade class an assignment; Get their parents to tell them a story with a moral at the end of it.

The next day the kids came back and one by one began to tell their stories.

'Tony, do you have a story to share?'

'Yes ma'am. My daddy told a story about my Aunt Karen. She was a pilot in Desert Storm and her plane got hit. She had to bail out over enemy territory and all she had was a flask of whiskey, a pistol and a survival knife. She drank the whiskey on the way down so it wouldn't break and then her parachute landed right in the middle of 20 enemy troops.

'She shot 15 of them with the gun until she ran out of bullets, killed four more with the knife, till the blade broke, and then she killed the last enemy with her bare hands.'

'Good Heavens,' said the horrified teacher. 'What kind of moral did your Daddy tell you from this horrible story?'

'Stay the f@#k away from Aunt Karen when she's drinking.'

243.

      I miss Bill Clinton. Yep, that's right . . . I miss Bill Clinton!

He was the closest thing the USA ever got to having a black man as President.

    1. He played the sax.

    2. He smoked weed.

    3. He had his way with ugly white women.

* Even now? Look at him . . . his wife works, and he doesn't! AND he gets a cheque from the government every month.

* Manufacturers announced today that they will be stocking America's shelves this week with 'Clinton Soup' in honour of one of the nations' most distinguished men. It consists primarily of a weenie in hot water.

* Chrysler Corporation is adding a new car to its line to honour Bill Clinton. The Dodge Drafter will be built in Canada.

* When asked what he thought about foreign affairs, Clinton replied; 'I don't know, I never had one.'

* Then Clinton revised the judicial oath; 'I solemnly swear to tell the truth as I know it, the whole truth as I believe it to be, and nothing but what I think you don't need to know.'

* Clinton will be recorded in history as the only President to do Hanky Panky between Bushes.

244.

There was this man and he went into the fruit shop and said; 'Can I have a kilo of tomatoes.'

The shop keeper said; 'Come back in a week so.'

He goes back the next day and says; 'Can I have a kilo of tomatoes.'

The shopkeeper says; 'Come back in a week.'

So he goes back the next day and says; 'Can I have a kilo of tomatoes.'

The shopkeeper says; 'What do you get if take the 'c' out of cat.'

'At.'

'What do you get if you take the 'd' out of dog.'

'Og.'

'What do you get if you take the 'f' out of tomatoes.'

'There's no 'f-in' tomatoes.'

'That's what I've been trying to tell you!'

245.

An Australian journalist in Jerusalem heard about an old Jewish man who'd been going to the Wailing Wall to pray, twice a day, every day, for 60 years.

She thought this would make a nice feel-good news item, so she went to the Wailing Wall to find the man.

After a short while, he arrived. She watched him pray for about 45 minutes and, when he turned to leave, she approached him for an interview.

'I'm Rebecca Smith from the Evening News, sir. How long have you been coming to the Wailing Wall and praying?'

'For about 60 years,' he replied slowly.

'That's amazing! What do you pray for?' she asks.

'I pray for peace between Christians, Jews and Muslims ma'am. I pray for all the hatred to stop and I pray for all our children to grow up in peace and friendship.'

'How do you feel after doing this for 60 years?' she enquires.

'Like I'm talking to a fricking brick wall!'

246.

There were two brother snakes which were very dangerous.

One day the stupider snake said to his brother; 'Are we dangerous. I mean are we poisonous?'

His brother looked at him in a weird way and then said; 'Yes, some of the most dangerous in the entire world. Why?'

'Because I just bit my tongue.'

247.

A man was walking down the street when he was accosted by a particularly dirty and shabby-looking homeless man who asked him for a couple of dollars for dinner.

The man took out his wallet, extracted $10 and asked; 'If I give you this money, will you buy some beer with it instead of dinner?'

'No, I had to stop drinking years ago,' the homeless man replied.

'Will you use it to go fishing instead of buying food?' the man asked.

'No, I don't waste time fishing,' the homeless man said. 'I need to spend all my time trying to stay alive.'

'Will you spend this on greens fees at a golf course instead of food?' the man asked.

'Are you NUTS!' replied the homeless man. 'I haven't played golf in 20 years!'

'Will you spend the money on a woman in the red light district instead of food?' the man continued.

'What disease would I get for 10 lousy bucks?' exclaimed the homeless man.

'Well,' said the man. 'I'm not going to give you the money. Instead, I'm going to take you home for a terrific dinner cooked by my wife.'

The homeless man was astounded.

'Won't your wife be furious with you for doing that? I know I'm dirty and I probably smell pretty disgusting.'

The man replied; 'That's okay. It's important for her to see what a man looks like after he has given up beer, fishing, golf and sex.'

248.

Once upon a time, in a nice little forest, there lived an orphaned bunny and an orphaned snake. By a surprising coincidence, both were blind from birth.

One day, the bunny was hopping through the forest, and the snake was slithering through the forest, when the bunny tripped over the snake and fell down. This, of course, knocked the snake about quite a bit.

'Oh, my,' said the bunny. 'I'm terribly sorry. I didn't mean to hurt you. I've been blind since birth, so I can't see where I'm going. In fact, since I'm also an orphan, I don't even know what I am.'

'It's quite ok,' replied the snake. 'Actually, my story is as yours. I too have been blind since birth, and also never knew my mother. Tell you what, maybe I could slither all over you, and work out what you are so at least you'll have that going for you.'

'Oh, that would be wonderful,' replied the bunny.

So the snake slithered all over the bunny, and said; 'Well, you're covered with soft fur, you have really long ears, your nose twitches, and you have a soft cottony tail. I'd say that you must be a bunny rabbit.'

'Oh, thank you, thank you,' cried the bunny, in obvious excitement.

The bunny suggested to the snake; 'Maybe I could feel you all over with my paw, and help you the same way that you've helped me.'

So the bunny felt the snake all over, and remarked; 'Well, you're smooth and slippery, and you have a forked tongue, no back-bone and no balls.

'I'd say you must be either a team leader, supervisor or possibly someone in senior management.'

249.

A kindergarten pupil told his teacher he'd found a cat, but it was dead.

'How do you know that the cat was dead?' she asked her pupil.

'Because I pissed in its ear and it didn't move,' answered the child innocently.

'You did WHAT?' the teacher exclaimed in surprise.

'You know,' explained the boy. 'I leaned over and went "Pssst!" and it didn't move.'

250.

A small boy is sent to bed by his father.

Five minutes later; 'Daaad.'

'What?'

'I'm thirsty. Can you bring a drink of water?'

'No, you had your chance before lights out.'

Five minutes later; 'Daaad.'

'WHAT?'

'I'm THIRSTY. Can I have a drink of water?'

'I told you NO! If you ask again, I'll have to spank you!'

Five minutes later; 'Daaad.'

'WHAT NOW!'

'When you come in to spank me, can you bring a drink of water?'

251.

An exasperated mother, whose son was always getting into mischief, finally asked him; 'How do you expect to get into Heaven?'

The boy thought it over and said; 'Well, I'll run in and out and in and out and keep slamming the door until St Peter says, "For Heaven's sake, Dylan, either come in or stay out!"'

252.

One summer evening during a violent thunderstorm a mother was tucking her son into bed. She was about to turn off the light when he asked with a tremor in his voice; 'Mommy, will you sleep with me tonight?'

The mother smiled and gave him a reassuring hug.

'I can't dear,' she said. 'I have to sleep in Daddy's room.'

A long silence was broken at last by his shaky little voice; 'The big sissy.'

253.   FATHER'S DAY

NEW EVENING CLASSES FOR MEN!!!

ALL ARE WELCOME

OPEN TO MEN ONLY – Husbands, Fathers, Boyfriends, Sons, Brothers

Note: Due to the complexity and level of difficulty, each course will accept a maximum of eight participants

The course covers two days, and topics covered in this course include:

DAY ONE

HOW TO FILL ICE CUBE TRAYS

Step by step guide with slide presentation

TOILET ROLLS – DO THEY GROW ON THE HOLDERS?

Roundtable discussion

DIFFERENCES BETWEEN LAUNDRY BASKET & FLOOR

Practising with hamper (Pictures and graphics)

DISHES & SILVERWARE – DO THEY LEVITATE/FLY TO KITCHEN SINK OR DISH-WASHER BY THEMSELVES?

Debate among a panel of experts

LOSS OF VIRILITY

Losing the remote control to your significant other – Help line and support groups

LEARNING HOW TO FIND THINGS

Starting with looking in the right place instead of turning the house upside down while screaming – Open forum

EMPTY MILK CARTONS – DO THEY BELONG IN THE FRIDGE OR THE BIN?

Group discussion and role play

HEALTH WATCH – BRINGING HER FLOWERS IS NOT HARMFUL TO YOUR HEALTH

PowerPoint presentation

REAL MEN ASK FOR DIRECTIONS WHEN LOST

Real life testimonial from the one man who did

IS IT GENETICALLY IMPOSSIBLE TO SIT QUIETLY AS SHE PARALLEL PARKS?

Driving simulation

LIVING WITH ADULTS – BASIC DIFFERENCES BETWEEN YOUR MOTHER AND YOUR PARTNER

Online class and role playing

HOW TO BE THE IDEAL SHOPPING COMPANION

Relaxation exercises, meditation and breathing techniques

REMEMBERING IMPORTANT DATES & CALLING WHEN YOU'RE GOING TO BE LATE

Bring your calendar or PDA to class

GETTING OVER IT – LEARNING HOW TO LIVE WITH BEING WRONG ALL THE TIME

Individual counsellors available

254.

It was that time, during the Sunday morning church service, for the children's sermon. All the children were invited to come forward.

One little girl was wearing a particularly pretty dress and, as she sat down, the pastor leaned over and said; 'That is a very pretty dress. Is it your Easter Dress?'

The little girl replied, directly into the pastor's clip-on microphone; 'Yes and my Mum says it's a bitch to iron.'

255.

A little boy was doing his math homework. He said to himself; 'Two plus five, that son of a bitch is seven. Three plus six, that son of a bitch is nine.'

His mother heard what he was saying and gasped; 'What are you doing?'

The little boy answered; 'I'm doing my math homework, Mum.'

'And this is how your teacher taught you to do it?' the mother asked.

'Yes,' he answered.

Infuriated, the mother asked the teacher the next day; 'What are you teaching my son in math?'

The teacher replied; 'Right now, we are learning addition.'

The mother asked; 'And are you teaching them to say two plus two, that son of a bitch is four?'

After the teacher stopped laughing, she answered; 'What I taught them was, two plus two, the sum of which, is four.'

256.
A certain little girl, when asked her name, would reply; 'I'm Mr Sugarbrown's daughter.'

Her mother told her this was wrong, she must say; 'I'm Jane Sugarbrown.'

The Vicar spoke to her in Sunday School and said, 'Aren't you Mr Sugarbrown's daughter?'

She replied; 'I thought I was, but mother says I'm not.'

257.
A little girl asked her mother; 'Can I go outside and play with the boys?'

Her mother replied; 'No, you can't play with the boys, they're too rough.'

The little girl thought about it for a few moments and asked; 'If I can find a smooth one, can I play with him?'

258.
A little girl goes to the barber shop with her father. She stands next to the barber chair, while her dad gets his hair cut, eating a cup cake.

The barber says to her; 'Sweetheart, you're going to get hair on your Twinkie.'

She says; 'Yes, I know, and I'm going to get boobs too.'

259.

My wife left me . . . I don't understand.

After the last child was born, she told me we had to cut back on expenses; I had to give up drinking beer. I was not a big drinker maybe a couple of 6-packs on weekends.

Anyway, I gave it up but I noticed the other day she came home from grocery shopping and when I looked at the receipt I noticed $45 in make-up.

I said; 'Wait a minute I've given up beer and you haven't given up anything!'

She said; 'I buy that make-up for you, so I can look pretty for you.'

I told her; 'Hell, that's what the beer was for!'

I don't think she'll be back.

260.

A circus owner runs an ad for a lion tamer and two people show up.

One is a good-looking, older retired navy chief in his mid-60s and the other is a gorgeous blonde in her mid-20s.

The circus owner tells them; 'I'm not going to sugar coat it. This is one ferocious lion. He ate my last tamer so you guys better be good or you're history. Here's your equipment . . . chair, whip and a gun. Who wants to try out first?'

The girl says; 'I'll go first'

She walks past the chair, the whip and the gun and steps right into the lion's cage. The lion starts to snarl and pant and begins to charge her.

About halfway there, she throws open her coat revealing her beautiful naked body. The lion stops dead in his tracks, sheepishly crawls up to her and starts licking her; feet and ankles. He continues to lick and kiss her entire body for several minutes and then rests his head at her feet.

The circus owner's mouth is on the floor.

He says; 'I've never seen a display like that in my life.'

He then turns to the retired chief and asks; 'Can you top that?'

The tough old chief replies; 'No problem, just get that lion out of the way.'

261. A guy went to his travel agent and tried to book a two-week cruise for himself and his lady friend. The travel agent said that all the ships were booked up and reservations were very tight at that moment, but that he would see what he could do.

A couple of days later, the travel agent phoned and said he could get them onto a three-day cruise. The guy was disappointed that it was such a short cruise, but booked it and went to the drugstore to buy sea sick pills and three condoms.

The next day, the agent called back and reported that he now could book a 5-day cruise.

The guy said; 'Great, I'll take it!'

He returned to the same pharmacy to buy two more sea sick pills and two more condoms.

The following day, the travel agent called yet again, and said he was delighted that he could offer them bookings on an 8-day cruise.

The guy was elated and, and went back to the chemist. He asked for three more sea sick pills and three more condoms.

The pharmacist looked sympathetically at him and said; 'Look, I'm not trying to pry. But, if it makes you sick why do you keep doing it?'

262.

A census taker in a rural area went up to a farmhouse and knocked on the door.

When a woman came to the door, he asked her how many children she had and their ages.

She said; 'Les' see now, there's the twins, Margie and Mikey, they're 18. And the twins, Pam and Sam, they're 16. And the twins, Sissy and Missy, they're 14.'

'Hold on!' said the census taker. 'Did you get twins every time?'

The woman answered; 'Heck no, there were hundreds of times we didn't get nothin'.'

263.

A bear, a lion and a chicken meet.

Bear says; 'If I roar in the forest, the entire forest shivers with fear.'

Lion says; 'If I roar in the desert, the entire desert is afraid of me.'

Says the chicken; 'Big deal I only have to cough, and the entire planet s@#ts itself.'

264.

A man entered the bus with both of his front pockets full of golf balls and sat down next to a beautiful (you guessed it) blonde. The puzzled blonde kept looking at him and his bulging pockets.

Finally, after many such glances from her he said, 'It's golf balls.'

Nevertheless, the blonde continued to look at him thoughtfully and finally, not being able to contain her curiosity any longer, asked, 'Does it hurt as much as tennis elbow?'

265.

UnDerstanDinG EnGineers . . . Take One

Two engineering students were walking across a university campus when one said; 'Where did you get such a great bike?'

The second engineer replied; 'Well, I was walking along yesterday, minding my own business, when a beautiful woman rode up on this bike, threw it to the ground, took off all her clothes and said; 'Take what you want.'

The first engineer nodded approvingly and said; 'Good choice; the clothes probably wouldn't have fitted you anyway.'

266.

UNDERSTANDING ENGINEERS . . . TAKE TWO

To the optimist, the glass is half-full.

To the pessimist, the glass is half-empty.

To the engineer, the glass is twice as big as it needs to be.

267.

UNDERSTANDING ENGINEERS . . . TAKE THREE

A priest, a doctor, and an engineer were waiting one morning for a particularly slow group of golfers.

The engineer fumed; 'What's with those guys? We must have been waiting for fifteen minutes!'

The doctor chimed in; 'I don't know, but I've never seen such inept golf!'

The priest said; 'Here comes the green-keeper. Let's have a word with him.'

He said; 'Hello George, what's wrong with that group ahead of us? They're rather slow, aren't they?'

The green-keeper replied; 'Oh, yes. That's a group of blind firemen. They lost their sight saving our clubhouse from a fire last year, so we always let them play for free anytime.'

The group fell silent for a moment.

The priest said, 'That's so sad. I think I will say a special prayer for them tonight.'

The doctor said; 'Good idea. I'm going to contact my ophthalmologist colleague and see if there's anything he can do for them.'

The engineer said; 'Why can't they play at night?'

268.
UNDERSTANDING ENGINEERS . . . TAKE FOUR

What is the difference between mechanical engineers and civil engineers?

Mechanical engineers build weapons and civil engineers build targets.

269.
UNDERSTANDING ENGINEERS . . . TAKE FIVE

The graduate with a science degree asks; 'Why does it work?'

The graduate with an engineering degree asks; 'How does it work?'

The graduate with an accounting degree asks; 'How much will it cost?'

The graduate with an arts degree asks; 'Do you want fries with that?'

PGA ASPIRATIONS . . . ?

Four lawyers in a law firm lived and died for their Saturday morning round of golf. It was their favourite moment of the week. Then one of the lawyers was transferred to an office in another city. It wasn't quite the same without him.

A new woman lawyer joined their law firm. One day she overheard the remaining three talking about their golf round at the coffee table.

Curious, she spoke up. 'You know, I used to play on my golf team at university and I was pretty good. Would you mind if I joined you next week?'

The three lawyers looked at each other. They were hesitant. Not one of them wanted to say 'yes', but she had them on the spot.

Finally one man said it would be okay, but they would be starting pretty early ... at 6.30am. He figured the early tee-off time would discourage her. The woman said this might be a problem and asked if she could possibly be up to 15 minutes late. They rolled their eyes but said this would be okay.

She smiled and said, 'Good, then I'll be there either at 6.30 or 6.45.'

She showed up right at 6.30 and wound up beating all three of them with an eye-opening 2-under par round. She was a fun and pleasant person the entire round. The guys were impressed!

Back in the clubhouse, they congratulated her and happily invited her back the next week.

She smiled and said, 'Sure, I'll be here at 6.30 or 6.45.'

The next week, she again showed up at 6.30 Saturday morning. Only this time, she played left-handed.

The three lawyers were incredulous as she still managed to beat them with an even par round despite playing with her off-hand. By now, the guys were totally amazed, but wondered if she was just trying to make them look bad by beating them left-handed.

They couldn't figure her out. She was again very pleasant and didn't seem to be showing them up, but each man began to harbour a burning desire to beat her!

In the third week, they all had their game faces on. But this week, she was 15 minutes late! This had the guys irritable because each was determined to play the best round of golf of his life to beat her. As they waited for her, they figured her late arrival was some petty gamesmanship on her part.

Finally she showed up. This week, the lady lawyer played right-handed which was a good thing since she narrowly beat all three of them.

However, she was so gracious and so complimentary of their strong play it was hard to keep a grudge against her. This woman was a riddle no-one could figure out!

Back in the clubhouse, she had all three guys shaking their heads at her ability. They had a couple of beers after their round which helped the conversation loosen up. Finally one of the men could contain his curiosity no longer.

He asked her point blank, 'How do you decide if you're going to golf right-handed or left-handed?'

The lady blushed and grinned.

She said, 'That's easy. When my Dad taught me to play golf, I learned I was ambidextrous. I have always had fun switching back and forth. Then when I met my husband in college and got married, I discovered he always sleeps in the nude.

'From then on, I developed a silly habit. Right before I left in the morning for golf practice, I would pull the covers off him. If his 'you-know-what' was pointing to the right, I golfed right-handed, and if it was pointing to the left, I golfed left-handed.'

All the guys on the team thought this was hysterical. Astonished at this bizarre information, one of the guys shot back, 'But what if it pointed straight up in the air?'

She said, 'Then I'm fifteen minutes late!'

211.
UnDerstanDinG EnGineers ... Take Six

Three engineering students were gathered together discussing who must have designed the human body.

One said; 'It was a mechanical engineer. Just look at all the joints.'

Another said; 'No, it was an electrical engineer. The nervous system has many thousands of electrical connections.'

The last one said; 'No, actually it had to have been a civil engineer. Who else would run a toxic waste pipeline through a recreational area?'

272.
UNDERSTANDING ENGINEERS ... Take Seven

Normal people believe that if it ain't broke, don't fix it.

Engineers believe that if it ain't broke, it doesn't have enough features yet.

273.
UNDERSTANDING ENGINEERS ... Take Eight

An engineer was crossing a road one day, when a frog called out to him and said; 'If you kiss me, I'll turn into a beautiful princess.'

He bent over, picked up the frog and put it in his pocket.

The frog spoke up again and said; 'If you kiss me I'll turn back into a beautiful princess and stay with you for one week.'

The engineer took the frog out of his pocket, smiled at it and returned it to the pocket.

The frog then cried out; 'If you kiss me and turn me back into a princess, I'll stay with you for one week and do ANYTHING you want.'

Again, the engineer took the frog out, smiled at it and put it back into his pocket.

Finally, the frog asked; 'What is the matter? I've told you I'm a beautiful princess and that I'll stay with you for one week and do anything you want. Why won't you kiss me?'

The engineer said; 'Look, I'm an engineer. I don't have time for a girlfriend, but a talking frog, now that's cool.'

274.
The husband and wife go to a counsellor after 15 years of marriage.

The counsellor asks them what the problem is and the wife goes into a tirade listing every problem they have ever had in the 15 years they've been married. She goes on and on and on.

Finally, the counsellor gets up, goes around the desk, embraces the woman and kisses her passionately, rips off her clothes and makes mad passionate love to her. Needless to say, the woman shuts up and then sits quietly with a very satisfied look on her face.

The counsellor turns to the husband and says; 'That is what your wife needs at least three times a week. Can you do that?'

The husband thinks for a moment and replies; 'Well, I can get her here Mondays and Wednesdays, but Fridays I play golf.'

275.
A firefighter was working on the fire engine outside the station when he noticed a little girl nearby in a little red wagon with little ladders hung off the sides and a garden hose tightly coiled in the middle.

The girl was wearing a firefighter's helmet, and the wagon was being pulled by her dog and her cat.

The firefighter walked over to take a closer look.

'That sure is a nice fire truck,' the firefighter said with admiration.

'Thanks,' the girl replied.

The firefighter looked a little closer and noticed the girl had tied the wagon to her dog's collar and to the cat's testicles.

'Little partner,' the firefighter said. 'I don't want to tell you how to run your rig, but if you were to tie that rope around the cat's collar, I think you could go faster.'

The little girl replied thoughtfully; 'You're probably right, but then I wouldn't have a siren.'

276.

I pulled into the crowded parking lot at the K-Mart Shopping Centre and rolled down the car windows to make sure my Labrador Retriever pup had fresh air.

She was stretched full-out on the back seat and I wanted to impress upon her that she must remain there. I walked to the curb backward, pointing my finger at the car and saying emphatically; 'Now you stay. Do you hear me? Stay! Stay!'

The driver of a nearby car, a pretty blonde young lady, gave me a strange look and said; 'Why don't you just put it in park?'

277.

A blonde walks into the police department looking for a job. The officer wants to ask her a few questions.

Officer: What's 2+2?

Blonde: Ummmmm . . . 4!

Officer: What's the square root of 100?

Blonde: Ummmm . . . 10!

Officer: Good! Now, who killed Abraham Lincoln?

Blonde: Ummmm . . . I dunno.

Officer: Well, you can go home and think about it. Come back tomorrow.

The blonde goes home and calls up one of her friends, who asks her if she got the job.

The blonde says, excitedly; 'Not only did I get the job, I'm already working on a murder case!'

218.

Q. How do you know if you're a pirate?

A. You don't, you just AARGH!

219.

Douglas the humble Crab and Kate the Lobster Princess were madly, deeply and passionately in love. For months they enjoyed an idyllic relationship until one day Kate scuttled over to Douglas in tears.

'We can't see each other any more,' she sobbed.

'Why?' gasped Douglas.

'Daddy says that crabs are too common,' she wailed. 'He claims you are a mere crab, a poor one at that, and crabs are the lowest class of crustacean and that no daughter of his will marry someone who can only walk sideways.'

Douglas was shattered and scuttled sideways away into the darkness to drink himself into a filthy state of aquatic oblivion.

That night, the great Lobster Ball was taking place. Lobsters came from far and wide, dancing and merry making, but the

Lobster Princess refused to
join in, choosing instead to sit
by her father's side in
inconsolable sorrow.

Suddenly the doors burst
open, and Douglas the
Crab strode in.

The lobsters all stopped their
dancing, the Princess gasped
and the King Lobster fell from his throne.

Slowly, painstakingly, Douglas the crab made his way across the
floor and all could see that he was walking, not sideways . . .
But FORWARD.

Yes FORWARDS! One claw after another!

Step by step he made his approach towards the throne, until he
looked the King Lobster in the eye.

There was a deadly hush . . . Finally, Douglas spoke . . .

'F@#k, I'm pissed.'

280.

Helen Clarke, Prime Minister of New Zulland, is rudely
awoken at 4am by the telephone.

'Hillen, it's the Hilth Munister here. Sorry to bother you at this
hour but there is an imirgincy! I've just received word thet the
Durex fectory en Auckland has burned to the ground. It is
istimated thet the entire New Zulland supply of condoms will
be gone by the ind of the week.'

PM: 'Shut. The economy wull niver be able to cope with all
those unwanted babies. Wi'll be ruined!'

Hilth Munister: 'We're going to hef to shup some in from abroad. . . Brutain?'

PM: 'No chence!! The Poms will have a field day on thus one!'

Hilth Munister: 'What about Australia?'

PM: 'Maybe – but we don't want them to know thet we are stuck.'

Hilth Munister: 'You call John Howard. Tell hum we need one moollion condoms; ten enches long and eight enches thuck! That way they'll know how bug the Kiwis really are!!'

Helen calls John, who agrees to help the Kiwis out in their hour of need. Three days later a ship arrives in Auckland – full of boxes.

A delighted Hillen rushes out to open the boxes. She finds condoms; ten enches long; eight enches thuck, all coloured green and gold. She then notices in small writing on each and ivery one.

Made in Australia – Size: MEDIUM

281.

Two baked beans went on Holiday to Queensland.

They both ended up in Cairns.

282.

A man on his way home from work comes to a dead halt in traffic and thinks to himself; 'This traffic seems worse than usual. Nothing is even moving.'

He notices a police officer walking back and forth between the lines of cars, so he rolls down his window and asks; 'Constable, what's the hold up?'

The constable replies, 'It's Eddie McGuire. He's just so depressed about his personal life – the thought of moving the wife and kids to Sydney and the state of disruption among his beloved Magpies, Channel 9 losing the football coverage, having to give up *The Footy Show*, *Who wants to be a Millionaire*, and his Triple M radio show, that he's stopped his motorcade in the middle of the freeway and he's threatening to douse himself in petrol and set himself on fire.

'He says his family hates him and he doesn't have the money to pay for the new house renovations at Point Piper and to bring his current house in Toorak up to scratch to put on the market. So we're taking up a collection for him.'

'Oh really? How much have you got so far?'

'About 300 litres, but a lot of people are still siphoning.'

283.

Why men have Better frienDs

Women's Friends: A woman didn't come home one night. The next day she told her husband that she had slept over at a friend's house.

The husband called his wife's ten best friends. None of them knew what he was talking about.

Men's Friends: A man didn't come home one night. The next day he told his wife that he had slept over at a friend's house.

The wife called her husband's ten best friends. Eight of them confirmed that he had slept over, and two claimed he was still there.

284.
There once was a Red Indian whose given name was Onestone, so named because he had only one testicle. He hated that name and asked everyone not to call him Onestone.

After years and years of torment, Onestone finally cracked and said; 'If anyone calls me Onestone again I will kill them!'

The word got around and nobody called him that any more.

Then one day a young woman named Blue Bird forgot and said; 'Good morning, Onestone.'

He jumped up, grabbed her and took her deep into the forest where he made love to her all day and all night. He made love to her all the next day, until Blue Bird died from exhaustion.

The word got around that Onestone meant what he promised he would do.

Years went by and no one dared call him by his given name until a woman named Yellow Bird returned to the village after being away for many years.

Yellow Bird, who was Blue Bird's cousin, was overjoyed when she saw Onestone. She hugged him and said; 'Good to see you, Onestone.'

Onestone grabbed her, took her deep into the forest, then he made love to her all day, made love to her all night, made love to her all the next day, made love to her all the next night, but Yellow Bird wouldn't die!

The moral of the story is: You can't kill two birds with one stone!!

285.

I went to the doctor this week for my yearly physical.

The nurse starts with certain basic items.

'How much do you weigh?' she asks.

'53 kg,' I said.

The nurse put me on the scales.

It turns out that I weigh 68 kg.

The nurse asks; 'Your height?'

'168 cm,' I said.

The nurse checks and sees that I only measure 160cm.

She then takes my blood pressure and tells me it is very high.

'Of course it's high!' I screamed, 'Look what you've gone and done to me! When I came in here I was tall and slender! Now I'm short and fat!'

286.

Miss Jones had been giving her second-grade students a lesson on science.

She had explained about magnets and showed how they would pick up nails and other bits of iron.

Now it was question time and she asked; 'My name begins with the letter M and I pick up things. What am I?'

A little boy on the front row said; 'You're a mother.'

287.

Olaf and Sven were fishing one day when Sven pulled out a cigar. Finding he had no matches, he asked Olaf for a light.

'Ya, shure, I tink I haff a lighter,' he replied.

Then reaching into his tackle box, he pulled out a Bic lighter ten inches long.

'Yiminy Cricket!' exclaimed Sven, taking the huge Bic lighter in his hands. 'Vere dit yew git dat monster??'

'Vell,' replied Olaf. 'I got it from my Genie.'

'You haff a Genie??' Sven asked.

'Ya, shure. It's right here in my tackle box,' says Olaf.

'Could I see him?'

Olaf opens his tackle box and sure enough, out pops the Genie.

Addressing the genie, Sven says, 'Hey dere! I'm a good friend of your master. Vill you grant me vun vish?'

'Yes, I will,' says the Genie.

So Sven asks the Genie for a million bucks.

The Genie disappears back into the tackle box leaving Sven sitting there, waiting for his million bucks. Shortly, the sky darkens and is filled with the sound of a million ducks flying overhead.

Over the roar of the million ducks Sven yells at Olaf; 'Yumpin' Yimminy!! I asked for a million bucks, not a million ducks!'

Olaf answers; 'Ya, I forgot to tell yew dat da Genie is hart of hearing. Do yew really tink I asked for a 10-inch Bic?'

288.

Patient said to the doctor; 'Don't laugh!'

'Of course, I won't laugh,' the doctor said. 'I'm a professional. In over 20 years I've never laughed at a patient.'

'Okay then,' the patient said, and proceeded to drop his trousers, revealing the tiniest 'whooha' the doctor had ever seen.

It couldn't have been bigger than the size of a triple A battery! Unable to control himself, the doctor started giggling, and then fell laughing to the floor. Ten minutes later he was able to struggle to his feet and regain his composure.

'I'm so sorry,' said the doctor. 'I really am. I don't know what came over me. On my honour as a doctor and a gentleman, I promise it won't happen again. Now what seems to be the problem?'

'It's swollen,' the patient replied.

289.

A nun, badly needing to use the restroom, walked into a local Hooters restaurant. The place was hopping with music and loud conversation and every once in a while the lights would turn off.

Each time the lights would go out, the place would erupt into cheers. However, when the revellers saw the nun, the room went dead silent.

She walked up to the bartender and asked; 'May I please use the restroom?'

The bartender replied; 'OK, but I should warn you that there is a statue of a naked man in there wearing only a fig leaf.'

'Well, in that case I'll just look the other way,' said the nun.

So, the bartender showed the nun to the back of the restaurant.

After a few minutes, she came back out, and the whole place stopped just long enough to give the nun a loud round of applause.

She went to the bartender and said; 'Sir, I don't understand. Why did they applaud for me just because I went to the restroom?'

'Well, now they know you're one of us,' said the bartender. 'Would you like a drink?'

'But, I still don't understand,' said the puzzled nun.

'You see,' laughed the bartender. 'Every time someone lifts the fig leaf on that statue, the lights go out.'

290.
The Smiths were unable to conceive children and decided to use a surrogate father to start their family.

On the day the proxy father was to arrive, Mr Smith kissed his wife goodbye and said; 'Well, I'm off now. The man should be here soon.'

Half an hour later, just by chance, a door-to-door baby photographer happened to ring the doorbell, hoping to make a sale.

'Good morning, Ma'am', he said. 'I've come to'. . .

'Oh, no need to explain,' Mrs Smith cut in, embarrassed. 'I've been expecting you.'

'Have you really?' said the photographer. 'Well, that's good. Did you know babies are my specialty?'

'Well that's what my husband and I had hoped. Please come in and have a seat.'

After a moment she asked, blushing; 'Well, where do we start?'

'Leave everything to me. I usually try two in the bathtub, one on the couch, and perhaps a couple on the bed. And sometimes the living room floor is fun. You can really spread out there.'

'Bathtub, living room floor? No wonder it didn't work out for Harry and me!'

'Well, Ma'am, none of us can guarantee a good one every time. But if we try several different positions and I shoot from six or seven angles, I'm sure you'll be pleased with the results.'

'My, that's a lot!' gasped Mrs Smith.

'Ma'am, in my line of work a man has to take his time. I'd love to be in and out in five minutes, but I'm sure you'd be disappointed with that.'

'Don't I know it,' said Mrs Smith quietly.

The photographer opened his briefcase and pulled out a portfolio of his baby pictures.

'This was done on the top of a bus,' he said.

'Oh my God!' Mrs Smith exclaimed, grasping at her throat.

'And these twins turned out exceptionally well when you consider their mother was so difficult to work with.'

'She was difficult?' asked Mrs Smith.

'Yes, I'm afraid so. I finally had to take her to the park to get the job done right. People were crowding around four and five deep to get a good look.'

'Four and five deep?' said Mrs Smith, her eyes wide with amazement.

'Yes', the photographer replied. 'And for more than three hours, too. The mother was constantly squealing and yelling. I could hardly concentrate, and when darkness approached I had to rush my shots. Finally, when the squirrels began nibbling on my equipment, I just had to pack it all in.

Mrs Smith leaned forward. 'Do you mean they actually chewed on your, uh . . . equipment?'

'It's true, Ma'am, yes. Well, if you're ready, I'll set-up my tripod and we can get to work right away.'

'Tripod?'

'Oh yes, Ma'am. I need to use a tripod to rest my Canon on. It's much too big to be held in the hand very long.'

And that's when Mrs Smith fainted . . .

291.

Shortly after the Pope had apologised to the Jewish people for the treatment of Jews by the Catholic Church over the years, Ariel Sharon then Prime Minister of Israel, sent a proposal to the College of Cardinals for a friendly game of golf to be played between the two leaders, or their representatives, to demonstrate the friendship and ecumenical spirit shared by the Catholics and the Jews.

The Pope met his College of Cardinals to discuss the proposal.

'Your Holiness,' said one of the Cardinals, 'Mr Sharon wants to challenge you to a game of golf to show that you are old and unable to compete. I am afraid that this would tarnish our image in the world.'

The Pope thought about this and, since he had never held a golf club in his life, asked; 'Don't we have a Cardinal to represent me?'

'None who plays golf very well,' a Cardinal replied. 'But there is a man named Jack Nicklaus, an American golfer, who is a devout Catholic. We could offer to make him a Cardinal, and then ask him to play Mr Sharon as your personal representative. In addition to showing our spirit of co-operation, we will also win the match.'

Everyone agreed that this was a great idea. The call was made. Of course, Nicklaus was honoured and he agreed to play as a representative of the Pope.

The day after the match, Nicklaus reported to the Vatican to inform the Pope of the result.

'This is Cardinal Nicklaus. I have some good news and some bad news, Your Holiness,' said the golfer.

'Tell me the good news, Cardinal Nicklaus, 'said the Pope.

'Well Your Holiness, I don't like to brag, but even though I have played some pretty terrific rounds of golf in my life, this was the best I have ever played by far. I must have been inspired from above. My drives were long and true, my irons were accurate and purposeful, and my putting was perfect. With all due respect, my play was truly miraculous.'

'How can there be bad news,' the Pope asked.

Nicklaus sighed; 'I lost by three strokes to Rabbi Tiger Woods.'

292.

A woman was having a passionate affair with an inspector from a pest-control company.

One afternoon they were carrying on in the bedroom together when her husband arrived home unexpectedly.

'Quick,' said the woman to the lover. 'Into the closet!' And she pushed him in the closet, stark naked.

The husband, however, became suspicious and after a search of the bedroom discovered the man in the closet.

'Who are you?' he asked him.

'I'm an inspector from Bugs-B-Gone,' said the exterminator.

'What are you doing in there?' the husband asked.

'I'm investigating a complaint about an infestation of moths,' the man replied.

'And where are your clothes?' asked the husband.

The man looked down at himself and said; 'The little bastards!'

293.

An elderly man walks into a confessional. The following conversation ensues:

Man: 'I am 92 years old, have a wonderful wife of 70 years, many children, grandchildren, and great grandchildren. Yesterday, I picked up two college girls, hitchhiking. We went to a motel, where I had sex with each of them three times.'

Priest: 'Are you sorry for your sins?'

Man: 'What sins?'

Priest: 'What kind of a Catholic are you?'

Man: 'I'm Jewish.'

Priest: 'Why are you telling me all this?'

Man: 'I'm 92 years old . . . I'm telling everybody!'

294.

A woman was helping her husband set up his computer and, at the appropriate point in the process, she told him that he would now need to enter a password. Something he could remember easily and will use each time he has to log on.

The husband was in a rather amorous mood and figured he would try for the shock effect to bring this to his wife's attention. So when the computer asked him to enter his password, he made it plainly obvious to his wife that he was keying in;

P. . . E. . . N. . . I. . . S. . .

His wife fell off her chair laughing when the computer replied:

---PASSWORD REJECTED. NOT LONG ENOUGH---

295.

Rules for Bedroom Golf

* Each player shall furnish his own equipment for play, normally one club and two balls.

* Play on a course which must be approved by the owner of the hole.

* Unlike outdoor golf, the object is to get the club in the hole and keep the balls out of the hole.

* For most effective play, the club should have a firm shaft. Course owners are permitted to check the shaft for firmness before play begins.

* Course owners reserve the right to restrict the length of the club to avoid damage to the hole.

* The object of the game is to take as many strokes as necessary until the course owner is satisfied that play is complete. Failure to do so may result in being denied permission to play on the course again.

* It is considered bad form to begin playing the hole immediately upon arrival at the course. The experienced player will normally take time to admire the entire course with special attention to the well formed bunkers.

* Players are cautioned not to mention other courses they have played or are currently playing to the owner of the course being played. Upset course owners have been known to damage a player's equipment for this reason.

* Players are encouraged to bring proper rain gear along, just in case.

* Players should assure themselves that their match has been properly scheduled, particularly when a new course is being played for the first time. Previous players have been known to become irate if they discover someone else is playing what they consider to be a private course.

* Players should not assume a course is in shape for play at all times. Some players may be embarrassed if they find the course is temporarily under repair. Players are advised to be extremely tactful in this situation. More advanced players will find alternate means of play when this is the case.

* Players are advised to obtain the course owners permission before attempting to play the back nine.

* Slow play is encouraged, however, players should be prepared to proceed at quicker pace, at least temporarily, at the course owner's request.

* It is considered outstanding performance, time permitting, to play the same hole several times in one match.

* The course owner will be the sole judge of who is the best player.

Hint: *Players are advised to think twice before considering membership at a given course. Additional assessments may be levied by the owner and the rules are subject to change. For this reason, many players prefer to continue to play several different courses.*

296.
In 2001 if you had bought $1,000 of One-Tel stock, it would now be worth about $9 to you as an unsecured creditor if you are lucky.

In 2002 if you had bought HIH stock, you would have about $6.50 left of the original $1,000.

In 2003, if you had gone overseas and bought ENRON you would have less than $5 left.

But, if you had purchased $1,000 worth of beer only one year ago, drank all the beer, then turned in the cans for the aluminum recycling price, you would have $24.

The moral of the story is: The best investment advice is to drink heavily and recycle.

297.

After having their eleventh child, an Irish couple decided that was enough as they could not afford a larger bed.

So the husband went to his doctor and told him that he and his wife didn't want to have any more children. The doctor told him there was a procedure called a vasectomy that would fix the problem but it was expensive.

A less costly alternative was to go home, get a firework, light it, put it in a beer can, then hold the can up to his ear and count to ten.

The husband said, 'B'God, Doctor! I may not be the smartest guy in the world, but I don't see how putting a firework in a beer can next to my ear is going to help me.'

'Trust me, it will do the job', said the doctor.

So the man went home, lit a banger and put it in a beer can.

He held the can up to his ear and began to count; '1, 2, 3, 4, 5,' at which point he paused, placed the beer can between his legs so he could continue counting on his other hand.

298.

On a group of beautiful deserted tropical islands in the middle of nowhere the following people are suddenly stranded by, as you might expect, a shipwreck:

2 Italian men and 1 Italian woman

2 French men and 1 French woman

2 German men and 1 German woman

2 Greek men and 1 Greek woman

2 English men and 1 English woman

2 Bulgarian men and 1 Bulgarian woman

2 Japanese men and 1 Japanese woman

2 Chinese men and 1 Chinese woman

2 American men and 1 American woman, and

2 Irish men and 1 Irish woman

One month later on these same absolutely stunningly beautiful desert (and deserted) islands in the middle of nowhere, the following things have occurred:

One Italian man killed the other Italian man for the Italian woman.

The two French men and the French woman are living happily together in a menage-a-trois.

The two German men have a strict weekly schedule of alternating visits with the German woman.

The two Greek men are sleeping with each other and the Greek woman is cleaning and cooking for them.

The two English men are waiting for someone to introduce them to the English woman.

The two Bulgarian men took one long look at the endless ocean, another long look at the Bulgarian woman, and started swimming.

The two Japanese men have faxed Tokyo and are awaiting instructions.

The two Chinese men have set up a pharmacy, a liquor store, a restaurant and a laundry, and have got the woman pregnant in order to supply employees for the stores.

The two American men are contemplating the virtues of suicide because the American woman keeps endlessly complaining about her body, the true nature of feminism, how she can do everything they can do, the necessity of fulfilment, the equal division of household chores, how sand and palm trees make her look fat, how her last boyfriend respected her opinion and treated her nicer than they do, how her relationship with her mother is improving, and at least the taxes are low and it isn't raining.

The two Irish men have divided the island into North and South and set up a distillery. They do not remember if sex is in the picture because it gets sort of foggy after the first few liters of coconut whiskey.

But they're happy because at least the English aren't having any fun.

299.

A man went to the Police Station wishing to speak with the burglar who had broken into his house the night before.

'You'll get your chance in court,' said the Desk Sergeant.

'No, no, no!' said the man. 'I want to know how he got into the house without waking my wife. I've been trying to do that for twenty years!'

300.

Every year Morris and his wife Esther went to the Royal Easter Show.

And each year Morris would say; 'Esther, I'd like a ride in that helicopter.'

Esther always replied; 'I know Morris, but that helicopter ride costs $50 and $50 is $50.'

Each year was the same until finally Morris and Esther were once again at the show and Morris turns to Esther and says; 'Esther, I'm 85 years old. If I don't get to ride in that helicopter now I might never get another chance.'

Esther replies; 'Morris, that helicopter ride costs $50 and $50 is $50.'

The pilot overheard the couple talking and said; 'Folks, I'll make you a deal. I'll take the both of you for a ride and if you can stay quiet for the entire ride and not say a word I won't charge you! But, if you say one word, it will cost $50 for the two of you.'

Morris and Esther agreed and up they went.

The pilot did all kinds of fancy maneuvers but not a word was heard. He did daredevil tricks over and over again but still not a word.

When they finally landed, the pilot turned to Morris and said; 'By golly I did everything I could to get you to yell out but you didn't, I'm very impressed!'

Morris replied; 'Well I was going to say something when Esther fell out. But $50 is $50.'

301.

An Australian ventriloquist visiting New Zealand, walks into a small village and sees a local sitting on his porch patting his dog.

He figures he'll have a little fun, so he says to the Kiwi; 'G'day, mind if I talk to your dog?'

Villager: 'The dog doesn't talk, you stupid Aussie.'

Ventriloquist: 'Hello dog, how's it going mate?'

Dog: 'Doin' all right.'

Kiwi: (look of extreme shock)

Ventriloquist: 'Is this villager your owner?'

Dog: 'Yep'

Ventriloquist: 'How does he treat you?'

Dog: 'Real good. He walks me twice a day, feeds me great food and takes me to the lake once a week to play.'

Kiwi: (look of utter disbelief)

Ventriloquist: 'Mind if I talk to your horse?'

Kiwi: 'Uh, the horse doesn't talk either . . . I think.'

Ventriloquist: 'Hey horse, how's it going?'

Horse: 'Cool '

Kiwi: (absolutely dumbfounded)

Ventriloquist: 'Is this your owner?'

Horse: 'Yep'

Ventriloquist: 'How does he treat you?'

Horse: 'Pretty good, thanks for asking. He rides me regularly, brushes me down often and keeps me in the barn to protect me from the elements.'

Kiwi: (total look of amazement)

Ventriloquist: 'Mind if I talk to your sheep?'

Kiwi: (in a panic) 'The sheep's a liar.'

302.

A couple goes for a meal at a Chinese restaurant and orders the 'Chicken Surprise'. The waiter brings the meal, served in a lidded cast iron pot.

Just as the wife is about to serve herself, the lid of the pot rises slightly and she briefly sees two beady little eyes looking around before the lid slams back down.

'Good grief, did you see that?' she asks her husband. He hadn't, so she asks him to look in the pot.

He reaches for it and again the lid rises, and he sees two little eyes looking around before it slams down.

Rather perturbed, he calls the waiter over, explains what is happening, and demands an explanation.

'Please sir,' says the waiter. 'What you order?'

The husband replies; 'Chicken Surprise.'

'Ah . . . so velly solly,' says the waiter, 'I bring you peeking-duck.'

303.
RUGBY's Offside rule explained to women

You're in a shoe shop, second in the queue for the till. Behind the shop assistant on the till is a pair of shoes which you have seen and which you must have.

The female shopper in front of you has seen them also and is eyeing them with desire. Both of you have forgotten your purses. It would be rude to push in front of the first woman if you had no money to pay for the shoes.

The shop assistant remains at the till waiting.

Your friend is trying on another pair of shoes at the back of the shop and sees your dilemma.

She prepares to throw her purse to you. If she does so, you can intercept the purse, then walk round the other shopper and buy the shoes!

At a pinch she could send the purse ahead of the other shopper and 'whilst it is in flight', you could nip around the other shopper, intercept the purse and buy the shoes!

BUT, you must always remember that until the purse has 'actually been thrown', it would be plain wrong for you to be in front of the other shopper and you would be OFFSIDE!

304.
A nurse walks into a bank totally exhausted after a 20-hour shift.

Preparing to write a cheque, she pulls a rectal thermometer out of her purse and tries to write with it.

KOChie's Best Jokes 2

She looks at the flabbergasted teller and without missing a beat says; 'Well, that's great . . . that's really great . . . some bum's got my pen.'

305.

Two patients limp into two different medical clinics with the same complaint. Both have trouble walking and appear to require a hip replacement.

The first patient is examined within the hour, is x-rayed the same day and has a time booked for surgery the following week.

The second sees his family doctor after waiting a week for an appointment, then waits 18 weeks to see a specialist Then gets an x-ray, which isn't reviewed for another month and finally has his surgery scheduled for a year from then.

Why the different treatment for the two patients?

The first is a Golden Retriever; the second is a Senior Citizen.

306.

A man who just died is delivered to the mortuary wearing an expensive, expertly tailored black suit.

The mortician asks the deceased's wife how she would like the body dressed. He points out that the man does look good in the black suit he is already wearing.

The widow, however, says that she always thought her husband looked his best in blue, and that she wants him in a blue suit.

She gives the mortician a blank cheque and says; 'I don't care what it costs, but please have my husband in a blue suit for the viewing.'

The woman returns the next day for the wake. To her delight, she finds her husband dressed in a gorgeous blue suit with a subtle chalk stripe. The suit fits him perfectly.

She says to the mortician; 'Whatever this cost, I'm very satisfied. You did an excellent job and I'm very grateful. How much did you spend?'

To her astonishment, the mortician says; 'There's no charge.'

'No, really, I must compensate you for the cost of that exquisite blue suit!' she says.

'Honestly, ma'am,' the mortician says. 'It cost nothing. You see, a deceased gentleman of about your husband's size was brought in shortly after you left yesterday, and he was wearing an attractive blue suit. I asked his wife if she minded him going to his grave wearing a black suit instead, and she said it made no difference as long as he looked nice'.

'So I just switched the heads.'

307.

A 90-year-old man said to his doctor; 'I've never felt better. I have an 18-year-old bride who is pregnant with my child. What do you think about that?'

The doctor considered his question for a minute and then said; 'I have an elderly friend who is a hunter and never misses a season. One day when he was going out in a bit of a hurry, he accidentally picked up his umbrella instead of his gun. When he got to the creek, he saw a duck sitting beside the stream. He raised his umbrella and went, bang, bang and the duck fell dead. What do you think of that?'

The 90-year-old said; 'I'd say somebody else shot that duck.'

The doctor replied; 'My point exactly . . . '

308.

A married couple went to the hospital to have their baby delivered.

Upon their arrival, the doctor said that the hospital was testing an amazing new high-tech machine that would transfer a portion of the mother's labour pain to the baby's father.

He asked if they were willing to try it out. Both said they were very much in favour of it.

The doctor set the pain transfer to 10 per cent for starters, explaining that even 10 per cent was probably more pain than the father had ever experienced before.

But as the labour progressed, the husband felt fine and asked the doctor to go ahead and kick it up a notch.

The doctor then adjusted the machine to 20 per cent pain transfer.

The husband was still feeling fine. The doctor then checked the husband's blood pressure and was amazed at how well he was doing.

At this point they decided to try for 50 per cent.

The husband continued to feel quite well.

Since the pain transfer was obviously helping the wife considerably, the husband encouraged the doctor to transfer ALL the pain to him.

The wife delivered a healthy baby with virtually no pain, and the husband had experienced none.

She and her husband were ecstatic.

When they got home, they found the milkman dead on the porch.

309.

      During the weeks before Amy's wedding, she was terribly anxious about making some mistakes at the ceremony. The minister reassured her several times, pointing out that the service was not difficult and she will do just fine.

'All you have to remember,' he said, 'is that when you enter the church you walk up the AISLE. The groom and best man will be waiting before the ALTAR. Then I shall request the congregation to sing a HYMN. Then we shall get on with the ceremony. All you have to remember is the order in which those things happen and you can't go wrong.'

The happy day finally arrived, and the bridegroom waited nervously for his bride to appear.

When she arrived and stood alongside him, he heard her quietly repeating to herself; 'Aisle, altar, hymn . . . aisle, altar, hymn.' ('I'll alter him!')

310.

      Based on statistics, the most used sexual position among married couples is 'Doggy Style'.

The husband sits and begs. While the wife rolls over and plays dead.

A farmer named Clyde had a car accident. In court, the trucking company's fancy lawyer was questioning Clyde.

'Didn't you say, "I'm fine" at the scene of the accident?' asked the lawyer.

Clyde responded, 'Well, I'll tell you what happened. I had just loaded my favourite horse, Bessie, into the . . .'

'I didn't ask for any details,' the lawyer interrupted. 'Just answer the question. Did you not say "I'm fine" at the scene of the accident?'

Clyde said, 'Well, I had just got Bessie into the trailer and I was driving down the road . . .'

The lawyer interrupted again and said, 'Judge, I am trying to establish the fact that, at the scene of the accident, this man told the Highway Patrolman on the scene that he was just fine. Now several weeks after the accident he is trying to sue my client. I believe he is a fraud. Please tell him to simply answer the question.'

By this time, the Judge was fairly interested in Clyde's answer and said to the lawyer, 'I'd like to hear what he has to say about his favourite nag Bessie.'

Clyde thanked the Judge and proceeded. 'Well as I was saying, I had just loaded Bessie, my favourite horse, into the trailer and was driving her down the highway when this huge semi-trailer ran the stop sign and smacked my truck right in the side. I was thrown into one ditch and Bessie was thrown into the other. I was hurting real bad and didn't want to move. However, I could hear ol' Bessie moaning and groaning. I knew she was in terrible shape just by her groans.

Shortly after the accident a Highway Patrolman came on the scene. He could hear Bessie moaning and groaning so he went over to her. After he looked at her, and saw her fatal condition, he took out his gun and shot her between the eyes.

'Then the Patrolman came across the road, gun still in hand, looked at me, and said, "How are you feeling?"'

'Now what the f@#k would you say?'

312.

A newlywed farmer and his wife were visited by her mother, who immediately demanded an inspection of the place.

The farmer genuinely tried to be friendly to his new mother-in-law, hoping that it could be a friendly, non-antagonistic relationship.

To no avail, she kept nagging them at every opportunity, demanding changes, offering unwanted advice, and making life unbearable for the farmer and his new bride.

While they were walking through the barn, the farmer's mule suddenly reared up and kicked the mother-in-law in the head, killing her instantly.

At the funeral service a few days later, the farmer stood near the casket and greeted folks as they walked by.

The pastor noticed that whenever a woman would whisper something to the farmer, he would nod his head and say something.

Whenever a man walked by and whispered to the farmer, however, he would shake his head and mumble a reply.

Very curious about this bizarre behavior, the pastor later asked the farmer what that was all about.

The farmer replied; 'The women would say, "What a terrible tragedy," and I would nod my head and say, "Yes, it was."

'The men would ask, "Can I borrow that mule?" and I would shake my head and say, "Can't. It's all booked up for a year."'

313.

Three elderly men are at the doctor's office for a memory test.

The doctor asks the first man; 'What is three times three?'

'274,' came the reply.

The doctor rolls his eyes and looks up at the ceiling, and says to the second man; 'It's your turn. What is three times three?'

'Tuesday,' replies the second man.

The doctor shakes his head sadly, then asks the third man; 'Okay, your turn. What's three times three?'

'Nine,' says the third man.

'That's great!' says the doctor. 'How did you get that?'

'Simple,' he says. 'Just subtract 274 from Tuesday.'

314.

Deep in the back woods of Letcher County, Kentucky, a hillbilly's wife went into labor in the middle of the night and the doctor was called out to assist in the delivery.

Since there was no electricity, the doctor handed the father-to-be a lantern and said; 'Here, you hold this high so I can see what I'm doing!'

Soon, a baby boy was brought into the world.

'Whoa there' said the doctor. 'Don't be in such a rush to put that lantern down. I think there's another one coming.

Sure enough, within minutes he had delivered a baby girl.

'Hold that lantern up! Don't set it down. There's another one!' said the doctor.

Within a few minutes he had delivered a third baby.

'No, don't be in a hurry to put down that lantern. It seems there's yet another one coming!' cried the doctor.

The redneck scratched his head in bewilderment, and asked the doctor; 'You don't reckon it might be the light that's attractin' 'em?'

315.

When girls don't put out!! This was written by a guy . . . it's pretty damn smart.

I never quite figured out why the sexual urge of men and women differ so much. And I never have figured out the whole Venus and Mars thing. I have never figured out why men think with their head and women with their heart.

For example: One evening last week, my girlfriend and I were getting into bed.

Well, the passion starts to heat up, and she eventually says; 'I don't feel like it, I just want you to hold me.'

I said; 'WHAT!! What was that?'

So she says the words that every boyfriend on the planet dreads to hear; 'You're just not in touch with my emotional needs as a woman enough for me to satisfy your physical needs as a man.'

She responded to my puzzled look by saying; 'Can't you just love me for who I am and not what I do for you in the bedroom?'

Realising that nothing was going to happen that night, I went to sleep.

The very next day I opted to take the day off of work to spend time with her. We went out to a nice lunch and then went shopping at a big, big unnamed department store. I walked around with her while she tried on several different very expensive outfits. She couldn't decide which one to take, so I told her we'd just buy them all.

She wanted new shoes to complement her new clothes, so I said; 'Lets get a pair for each outfit.'

We went on to the jewellery department where she picked out a pair of diamond earrings.

Let me tell you . . . she was so excited. She must have thought I was one wave short of a shipwreck.

I started to think she was testing me because she asked for a tennis bracelet when she doesn't even know how to play tennis.

I think I threw her for a loop when I said; 'That's fine, honey.'

She was almost nearing sexual satisfaction from all of the excitement.

Smiling with excited anticipation, she finally said; 'I think this is all dear, let's go to the check-out.'

I could hardly contain myself when I blurted out; 'No honey, I don't feel like it.'

Her face just went completely blank as her jaw dropped with a baffled; 'WHAT?'

I then said; 'Honey! I just want you to HOLD this stuff for a while. You're just not in touch with my financial needs as a man enough for me to satisfy your shopping needs as a woman.'

And just when she had this look like she was going to kill me, I added; 'Why can't you just love me for who I am and not for the things I buy you?'

Apparently I'm not having anything tonight either . . . but at least she knows I'm smarter than her.

316.

> **Q:** Where can women over the age of 50 find young, sexy men, who are interested in them?

A: Try a bookstore under fiction.

317.

> **Q:** What can a man do while his wife is going through menopause?

A: Keep busy. If you're handy with tools, you can finish the basement. When you are done you will have a place to live.

318.

> **Q:** How can you increase the heart rate of your 50+ year old husband?

A: Tell him you're pregnant.

319.

There was a lady at a bar. Every time she wanted a drink she would raise her hand. She had very bad armpit hair.

The bartender was getting really grossed out and told the man sitting at the bar that next time she did that he was not going to give her a drink.

One minute later she said, 'Bartender, bartender, get me another drink.'

The bartender said, 'No.'

A man sitting at the bar said, 'Oh give the poor ballerina another drink.'

The bartender said, 'How do you know she is a ballerina?'

The man replied, 'Well anyone who can lift their leg that high must be a ballerina!'

320.

Q: How can you avoid spotting a wrinkle every time you walk by a mirror?

A: The next time you're in front of a mirror, take off your glasses.

321.

Q: Why should 50+ year old people use valet parking?

A: Valets don't forget where they park your car.

322.
A very shy guy goes into a bar and sees a beautiful woman sitting at the bar. After an hour of gathering up his courage he finally goes over to her and asks, tentatively, 'Um, would you mind if I chatted with you for a while?' She responds by yelling, at the top of her lungs, 'No, I won't sleep with you tonight . . . you pig!'

Everyone in the bar is now staring at them. Naturally, the guy is hopelessly and completely embarrassed and he slinks back to his table with a red face. After a few minutes, the woman walks over to him and apologises.

She smiles at him and says, 'I'm sorry if I embarrassed you. You see, I'm a graduate student in psychology and I'm studying how people respond to embarrassing public situations.'

To which he responds, screaming at the top of his lungs, 'What do you mean $200 for a BJ?'

323.
Q: Is it common for 50+ year olds to have problems with short-term memory storage?

A: Storing memory is not a problem, retrieving it is a problem.

324.
Q: As people age, do they sleep more soundly?

A: Yes, but usually in the afternoon.

325.

Q: Where do 50+ year olds look for fashionable glasses?

A: Their foreheads.

326.

A man was out of town on business. While sitting around his hotel he became bored. So he thought to himself, 'Hmm, a beer would be really nice right now.' So he began to wander the streets of the unfamiliar city, looking for a bar. And, after a few minutes he came across one. He casually went inside and took a seat at the bar.

The bartender walks up and asks the man what he is drinking. Anxiously, the man says, 'Bud Light, please.'

The bartender then asked what the name of his penis was. The man looked at him with confusion and said, 'What are you talking about? All I want is a Bud Light and, besides, I have no name for my penis.'

The bartender, calming the man, said, 'Look around, all you see is men. That is because this is a gay bar. And the tradition is, when you order a drink, you state the name of your penis. Then I'll serve you a drink.'

The man, really thirsty for a beer, now says, 'Fine. Give me couple of minutes to think, and I'll order when I come up with something.'

So he is thinking about it for a couple of minutes and still can't come up with anything. So he decides to ask the guy next to him for an idea. The man states, in a feminine voice, 'Well I call mine Timex, because it takes a lickin' and keeps on tickin.'

The man quickly turns away and asks the man to his right. That man states in a deep, gruff voice, 'I call my Ford, because it is built ram tough. Have you driven a Ford lately?'

Again, the man quickly turns away. Then, suddenly he says, 'Bartender, come here, I am ready to order.'

The bartender says, 'What'll ya have?'

The man says, 'A Bud Light, please.'

The bartender asks, 'What is the name of your penis?'

The man responds, 'Secret . . . strong enough for a man but made for a woman.'

327.
    Q: What is the most common remark made by 50+ year olds when they enter antique stores?

A: 'I remember these.'

328.
    Humans originally existed as members of small bands of nomadic hunter/gatherers. They lived on deer in the mountains during the summer and would go to the coast and live on fish and lobster in the winter.

The two most important events in all of history were the invention of beer and the invention of the wheel. The wheel was invented to get man to the beer. These were the foundation of modern civilization and together were the catalyst for the splitting of humanity into two distinct subgroups: Liberals and Conservatives.

Once beer was discovered, it required grain and that was the beginning of agriculture. Neither the glass bottle nor aluminium can were invented yet, so while our early humans were sitting around waiting for them to be invented, they just stayed close to the brewery.

That's how villages were formed.

Some men spent their days tracking and killing animals to BBQ at night while they were drinking beer. This was the beginning of what is known as the Conservative movement.

Other men who were weaker and less skilled at hunting learned to live off the conservatives by showing up for the nightly B-B-Q's and doing the sewing, fetching, and hair dressing. This was the beginning of the Liberal movement.

Some of these Liberal men eventually evolved into women. The rest became known as girliemen.

Some noteworthy Liberal achievements include the domestication of cats, the invention of group therapy, group hugs, and the concept of Democratic voting to decide how to divide the meat and beer that Conservatives provided.

Over the years Conservatives came to be symbolised by the largest, most powerful land animal on earth, the elephant.

Liberals are symbolised by the jackass.

Modern Liberals like imported beer (with lime added), but most prefer white wine or imported bottled water. They eat raw fish but like their beef well done. Sushi, tofu, and French food are standard Liberal fare.

Another interesting evolutionary side note: most of their women have higher testosterone levels than their men. Most social workers, personal injury attorneys, journalists, dreamers in Hollywood and group therapists are Liberals.

Conservatives drink domestic beer. They eat red meat and still provide for their women. Conservatives are big-game hunters, rodeo cowboys, lumberjacks, construction workers, firemen, medical doctors, police officers, corporate executives, athletes, mariners and, generally, anyone who works productively.

Conservatives who own companies hire other conservatives who want to work for a living.

Liberals produce little or nothing. They like to govern the producers and decide what to do with the production. Liberals believe Europeans are more enlightened than Americans. That is why most of the Liberals remained in Europe when Conservatives were coming to America. They crept in after the Wild West was tamed and created a business of trying to get more for nothing.

Here ends today's lesson in world history: It should be noted that a Liberal may have a momentary urge to angrily respond to the above before forwarding it. A Conservative will simply laugh and be so convinced of the absolute truth of this history that it will be forwarded immediately to other true believers and to more Liberals just to TEE them off.

HOW to shower like a woman

Take off clothes and place them sectioned in the laundry basket according to lights and darks. Walk to bathroom wearing long dressing gown. If you see husband along the way, cover up any exposed areas. Look at your womanly physique in the mirror . . . make mental note to do more sit-ups/leg-lifts etc.

Get in the shower. Use face cloth, arm cloth, leg cloth, long loofah, wide loofah and Pumice stone. Wash your hair once with cucumber and sage shampoo with 43 added vitamins. Wash your hair again to make sure it is clean.

Condition your hair with conditioner enhanced with grapefruit and mint. Wash your face with crushed apricot facial scrub for ten minutes until red. Wash entire rest of body with ginger nut and jaffa cake body wash. Rinse conditioner off hair. Shave armpits and legs. Turn off shower. Squeegee off all wet surfaces in shower. Spray mould spots with tile cleaner. Get out of shower. Dry with towel the size of a small country. Wrap hair in a super absorbent towel. Return to bedroom wearing long dressing gown and then hand towel on head. If you see your husband along the way, cover up any exposed areas.

HOW to shower like a man

Take off clothes while sitting on the edge of the bed and leave in a pile on the floor. Walk naked to the bathroom. If you see your wife along the way, shake willy at her making the 'woo-woo' sound. Look at your manly physique in the mirror. Admire the size of your willy and scratch your bum. Get in the shower. Wash your face. Wash your armpits. Blow your nose in your hands and let the water rinse it off. Fart and laugh at how loud it sounds in the shower.

Spend majority of time washing privates and surrounding area. Wash your bum, leaving those coarse bum hairs stuck on the soap. Wash your hair. Make a Shampoo Mohawk. Wee. Rinse off and get out of shower. Partially dry off. Fail to notice water on floor because curtain was hanging out of bath the whole time. Admire willy size in mirror again. Leave shower curtain open, wet mat on floor, light and fan on. If you pass wife, pull off towel, shake willy at her and make the 'woo-woo' sound again. Throw wet towel on bed.

I know you're laughing now because most of it is true!!!

330.

A guy was trying to console a friend who'd just found his wife in bed with another man.

'Get over it, buddy,' he said. 'It's not the end of the world.'

'It's all right for you to say,' answered his buddy. 'But what if you came home one night and caught another man in bed with your wife?'

The fella ponders for a moment, then says, 'I'd break his cane and kick his seeing-eye dog in the ass.'

331.

'Will the father be present during the birth?' asked the obstetrician.

'Nah,' replied the mother-to-be, 'he and my husband don't get along.'

332.

Q: Why do bagpipe players walk while they play?

A: To get away from the noise.

333.

A very successful lawyer parked his brand-new Lexus in front of his office, ready to show it off to his colleagues. As he got out, a truck passed too close and completely tore the door off of the driver's side. The counsellor immediately grabbed his mobile, dialled 000 and within minutes a policeman pulled up.

Before the officer had a chance to ask any questions, the lawyer started screaming hysterically. His Lexus, which he had just picked up the day before, was now completely ruined and would never be the same, no matter what the body shop did to it.

When the lawyer finally wound down from his ranting and raving, the officer shook his head in disgust and disbelief.

'I can't believe how materialistic you lawyers are,' he said. 'You are so focused on your possessions that you don't notice anything else.'

'How can you say such a thing?' asked the lawyer.

The cop replied, 'Don't you know that your left arm is missing from the elbow down? It must have been torn off when the truck hit you.'

'Ahhh!' screamed the lawyer. 'Where's my Rolex!'

334.

A teacher, a thief and a lawyer all die in the same freak accident. So when they reach the pearly gates, St Peter tells them that, unfortunately, heaven is overcrowded, so they each have to answer a question correctly for admission.

The teacher is first, and St Peter asks, 'Name the famous ship that was sunk by an iceberg?'

'Phew, that one's easy,' says the teacher, 'The Titanic.'

'Alright,' said St Peter, 'you may pass.'

Then the thief got his question: 'How many died on the Titanic?'

The thief replied, 'That's a toughy, but fortunately I just saw the movie. The answer is 1500 people.' And so he passed through.

Last, St Peter gave the lawyer his question: 'Name them.'

335. Two weeks ago was my 45th birthday, and I wasn't feeling too hot that morning anyway. I went to breakfast knowing my wife would be pleasant and say 'Happy Birthday,' and probably have a present for me.

She didn't even say 'Good Morning,' alone any 'Happy Birthday.' I thought, 'Well, that's wives for you. Maybe the children will remember.'

The children came in to breakfast and didn't say a word.

As I left for the office I was feeling pretty low and despondent. As I walked into my office, my secretary, Janet, said, 'Good morning boss, Happy Birthday.' And I felt a little better; someone had remembered.

I worked until noon. Then Janet knocked on my door and said, 'You know, it's such a beautiful day outside and it's your birthday, let's go to lunch, just you and me.' I said, 'By George, that's the best thing I've heard all day. Let's go.'

We went to lunch. We didn't go where we normally go; we went out into the country to a little private place. We had two martinis and enjoyed lunch tremendously.

On the way back to the office, she said, 'You know, it's such a beautiful day. We don't need to go back to the office, do we?' I said, 'No, I guess not.' She said, 'Let's go to my apartment.'

After arriving at her apartment she said, 'Boss, if you don't mind, I think I'll go into the bedroom and slip into something more comfortable.'

'Sure,' I excitedly replied. She went into the bedroom and, in about six minutes, she came out carrying a big birthday cake, followed by my wife, children and dozens of our friends. All were singing 'Happy Birthday' and there on the couch I sat . . . naked.

336.

A man comes home with his little daughter, whom he had taken to work for the day. The little girl asks, 'I saw you in your office with your secretary. Why do you call her a doll?'

Feeling his wife's gaze upon him, the man explains, 'Well, honey, my secretary is a very hard-working girl. She types like you wouldn't believe, she knows the computer system and is very efficient.'

'Oh,' says the little girl, 'I thought it was because she closed her eyes when you lay her down on the couch.'

337.

A woman arrives home from work and her husband notices she's wearing a diamond necklace. He asks his wife, 'Where did you get that necklace?'

She replies, 'I won it in a raffle at work. Go get my bath ready while I start dinner.'

The next day, the woman arrives home from work wearing a diamond bracelet. Her husband asks, 'Where did you get the bracelet?'

She replies, 'I won it in a raffle at work. Go get my bath ready while I start dinner.'

The next day, her husband notices she arrives home from work wearing a mink coat. He says, 'I suppose you won that in a raffle at work?'

She replies, 'Yeah I did! How did you guess? Go get my bath ready while I start supper.'

Later after supper, she goes to take her bath and she notices there is only one inch of water in the tub. She yells to her husband, 'HEY! There's only an inch of water in the tub.'

He replies, 'Yeah, I didn't want you to get your raffle ticket wet.'

338. A BaD Day!

* Well, this day was a total waste of make-up.

* Make yourself at home! Clean my kitchen.

* A hard-on doesn't count as personal growth.

* Don't bother me. I'm living happily ever after.

* Do I look like a friggin' people person?

* This isn't an office. It's Hell with fluorescent lighting.

* I started out with nothing and still have most of it left.

* I pretend to work. They pretend to pay me.

* If I throw a stick, will you leave?

* You! Off my planet!

* I like cats, too. Let's exchange recipes.

* Ambivalent? Well, yes and no.

* Did the aliens forget to remove your anal probe?

* Whatever kind of look you were going for, you missed.

* Suburbia: Where they tear out the trees and then name streets after them.

* Do they ever shut up on your planet?

* I'm just working here till a good fast-food job opens up.

* Are those your eyeballs? I found them in my cleavage.

* I'm not your type. I'm not inflatable.

* I'm trying to imagine you with a personality.

* A cubicle is just a padded cell without a door.

* Stress is when you wake up screaming and you realise you haven't fallen asleep yet.

* Don't worry. I forgot your name, too!

* Adults are just kids who owe money.

* You say I'm a bitch like it's a bad thing.

* Nice perfume. Must you marinate in it?

* Too many freaks, not enough circuses.

* Chaos, panic, and disorder – my work here is done.

* If I wanted to hear the pitter patter of little feet, I'd put shoes on my cat.

* You look like shit. Is that the style now?

* Earth is full. Go home.

* Is it time for your medication or mine?

* Does this condom make me look fat?

* I plead contemporary insanity.

* And which dwarf are you?

* I thought I wanted a career; turns out I just wanted pay cheques.

* How do I set a laser printer to stun?

* Meandering to a different drummer.

* I'm not tense, just terribly, terribly alert.

* I majored in liberal arts. Will that be for here or to go?

339.

There was a blonde driving down the road one day. She glanced to her right and noticed another blonde sitting in a nearby field, rowing a boat with no water in sight.

The blonde angrily pulled her car over and yelled at the rowing blonde, 'What do you think you're doing? It's things like this that give us blondes a bad name. If I could swim, I'd come out there and kick your butt!'

340.

A girl asks her boyfriend to come over Friday night and have dinner with her parents. Since this is such a big event, the girl tells him that after dinner, she would like to have sex with him for the first time.

The boy is ecstatic, but he has never had sex before, so he takes a trip to the pharmacy to get some condoms. The pharmacist helps the boy for about half an hour. He tells the boy everything there is to know about condoms and sex. At the register, the pharmacist asks the boy how many condoms he'd like to buy a 3-pack, 10-pack or family pack. The boy insists on the family pack because he thinks he will be rather busy, it being his first time and all.

That night, the boy shows up at the girl's parents' house and meets his girlfriend at the door. 'Oh, I'm so excited for you to meet my parents! Come on in!'

The boy goes inside and is taken to the dinner table where the girl's parents are seated. The boy quickly offers to say grace and bows his head. A minute passes, and the boy is still deep in prayer, with his head down. Ten minutes pass, and still no movement from the boy. Finally, after 20 minutes with his head down, the girlfriend leans over and whispers to the boyfriend,

'I had no idea you were this religious.'

The boy turns, and whispers back, 'I had no idea your father was a pharmacist!'

341. Every year, Bob goes hunting during bear season. One year, Bob shoots a small brown bear. Then, the mother of that small brown bear comes up to him and says, 'I'll give you two choices, I'll either kill you, or make love to you, but I won't let you go.'

Bob thinks on this, and decides he wants to live, so the mother bear then makes love to him.

The next year, Bob goes hunting again, but this time, he shoots the mother bear that he was forced to make love to the year before. He shoots her, and then her mother comes after Bob, and again, gives him the choice. 'I will make love to you, or kill you, which will it be??'

Again, Bob makes love to a bear.

The next year, Bob goes once again for revenge, and kills the bear that he was forced to make love to the year before.

This time, her sister comes up to Bob and says, 'You really don't come here for the hunting, do you?'

342. Did you hear about the near-tragedy at the mall? There was a power outage, and twelve blondes were stuck on the escalators for over four hours.

343.

Sam and Bessie are senior citizens, and Sam has always wanted an expensive pair of alligator cowboy boots. Seeing them on sale one day, he buys a pair and wears them home, asking Bessie, 'So, do you notice anything different about me?'

'What's different? It's the same shirt you wore yesterday and the same pants.'

'What's different?' Frustrated, Sam goes into the bathroom, undresses and comes out completely naked, wearing only his new boots. Again he says, 'Bessie, do you notice anything different?'

'What's different, Sam? It's hanging down today; it was hanging down yesterday and will be hanging down again tomorrow.'

Angrily, Sam yells, 'Do you know why it's hanging down? Cause it's looking at my new boots!!'

Bessie replies, 'You shoulda bought a hat!'

344.

'I think I have a problem, Doc,' says a patient. 'One of my balls has turned blue.'

The doctor examines the man briefly and concludes that the patient will die if he doesn't have his testicle removed.

'Are you crazy?!' bursts the patient. 'How could I let you do such a thing to me!'

'You want to die?' asks the doctor rhetorically, at which point the patient has to agree to have his testicle removed.

Two weeks after the operation, the patient comes back. 'Doc, I don't know how to say this, but the other ball has turned blue, too.'

Again, the doctor tells him that if he wants to live, his other testicle must be cut off, too. Again, the man is very reluctant to the idea.

'Hey, you want to die?' asks the doctor, and the patient has to agree with the operation. After two weeks of being testicle-less, the patient returns to the doctor and says, 'I think something is very wrong with me. My penis is now completely blue.'

After briefly examining the patient, the doctor gives him the bad news: If he wants to live, his penis has to go. Of course, the patient does not want to hear about it.

'You want to die?' asks the doctor.

'But . . . how do I pee?'

'We'll install a plastic pipe, and there will be no problem.'

So the patient has his penis removed, and, a while after the operation, the unfortunate man enters the doctor's office again. He is very angry.

'Doctor, the plastic pipe turned blue!'

'What?'

'Can you tell me what the hell is happening??'

The doctor examines the patient more carefully and says, 'Hmmm, I don't know. Could it be the tight blue jeans?'

345.

Three men were standing in line to get into Heaven one day. Apparently it had been a pretty busy day, though, so St Peter had to tell the first one, 'Heaven's getting pretty close to full today, and I've been asked to admit only people who have had particularly horrible deaths. So what's your story?'

The first man replies: 'Well, for a while I've suspected my wife has been cheating on me, so today I came home early to try to catch her red-handed. As I came into my 25th floor apartment, I could tell something was wrong, but all my searching around didn't reveal where this other guy could have been hiding. Finally, I went out to the balcony, and sure enough, there was this man hanging off the railing, 25 floors above ground! By now I was really mad, so I started beating on him and kicking him, but wouldn't you know it, he wouldn't fall off. So finally I went back into my apartment and got a hammer and starting hammering on his fingers. Of course, he couldn't stand that for long, so he let go and fell – but even after 25 stories, he fell into the bushes, stunned but okay. I couldn't stand it anymore, so I ran into the kitchen, grabbed the fridge, and threw it over the edge where it landed on him, killing him instantly. But all the stress and anger got to me, and I had a heart attack and died there on the balcony.'

'That sounds like a pretty bad day to me,' said St Peter, and let the man in.

The second man comes up and St Peter explains to him about Heaven being full, and again asks for his story.

'It's been a very strange day. You see, I live on the 26th floor of my apartment building, and every morning I do my exercises out on my balcony. Well, this morning I must have slipped or something, because I fell over the edge. But I got lucky, and caught the railing of the balcony on the floor below me. I knew I couldn't hang on for very long, when suddenly this man burst out onto the balcony. I thought for sure I was saved, when he started beating on me and kicking me. I held on the best I could until he ran into the apartment and grabbed a hammer and started pounding on my hands. Finally I just let go, but again I got lucky and fell into the bushes below, stunned but all right. Just when I was thinking I was going to be okay, this refrigerator comes falling out of the sky and crushes me instantly, and now I'm here.'

Once again, St Peter had to concede that that sounded like a pretty horrible death.

The third man came to the front of the line, and again the whole process was repeated. St Peter explained that Heaven was full and asked for his story.

'Picture this,' says the third man, 'I'm hiding naked inside a refrigerator . . .'

346.
      A blind man walks into a restaurant and sits down. The waiter, who is also the owner, walks up to the blind man and hands him a menu.

'I'm sorry, sir, but I am blind and can't read the menu. Just bring me a dirty fork from a previous customer. I'll smell it and order from there.'

A little confused, the owner walks over to the dirty dish pile and picks up a greasy fork. He returns to the blind man's table and hands it to him. The blind man puts the fork to his nose and takes in a deep breath.

'Ah, yes, that's what I'll have . . . meatloaf and mashed potatoes.'

Unbelievable, the owner thinks as he walks towards the kitchen. The cook happens to be the owner's wife. He tells her what had just happened. The blind man eats his meal and leaves.

Several days later, the blind man returns and the owner mistakenly brings him a menu again.

'Sir, remember me? I'm the blind man.'

'I'm sorry, I didn't recognise you. I'll go get you a dirty fork.'

The owner retrieves a dirty fork and brings it to the blind man. After another deep breath, the blind man says, 'That smells great. I'll take the macaroni and cheese with broccoli.'

Walking away in disbelief, the owner thinks the blind man is screwing around with him and tells his wife that the next time the blind man comes in he's going to test him.

The blind man eats and leaves.

He returns the following week, but this time the owner sees him coming and runs to the kitchen.

He tells his wife, 'Mary, rub this fork on your panties before I take it to the blind man.'

Mary complies and hands her husband the fork. As the blind man walks in and sits down, the owner is ready and waiting.

'Good afternoon, sir, this time I remembered you and I already have the fork ready for you.'

The blind man puts the fork to his nose, takes a deep whiff, and says, 'Hey I didn't know that Mary worked here . . . '

347.
     A couple returned from their honeymoon and it's obvious to everyone that they are not talking to each other. The groom's best man takes him aside and asks what is wrong.

'Well,' replied the man, 'When we had finished making love on the first night, as I got up to go to the bathroom I put a $50 bill on the pillow without thinking.'

'Oh, you shouldn't worry about that too much,' said his friend. 'I'm sure your wife will get over it soon enough – she can't expect you to have been saving yourself all these years!'

The groom nodded gently and said, 'I don't know if I can get over this though. She gave me $20 change!'

348.

The scene is a dark jungle. Two tigers are stalking through the undergrowth in single file when the one to the rear reaches out with his tongue and licks the bottom of the tiger in front. The startled tiger turns around and says, 'Hey! Cut it out, all right!'

The rear tiger says, 'Sorry,' and they continue. After about another five minutes, the rear tiger again reaches out with his tongue and licks the bottom of the tiger in front. The front tiger turns around and cuffs the rear tiger and says, 'I said stop it!'

The rear tiger says, 'Sorry,' and they continue. After about another five minutes, the rear tiger once more licks the bottom of the tiger in front. The front tiger turns around and asks the rear tiger, 'What is it with you, anyway?'

The rear tiger replies, 'Well, I just ate a lawyer and I'm trying to get the taste out of my mouth!'

349.

The Roadrunner was feeling very amorous one day, and since there were no other female roadrunners around, he decided to look around.

He happened to spot a lovely dove. Bzzzzzz . . . and down he goes and feathers are flying, lots of dust in the air and the dazed dove is lying there with a smile and says, 'I'm a dove and I've been loved!'

The Roadrunner is still not satisfied. He spots a Lark flying around and zooms down on her. Again, feathers are flying around and dust is in the air and the dazed Lark is lying there and said, 'I'm a Lark and I've been sparked.'

The Roadrunner is still not satisfied and spots a Duck. He zooms down and again feathers are flying and a lot of squawking and dust flying in the air, and the Roadrunner takes off.

The Duck is lying there really pissed off, and says 'I'm a Drake and there's been a mistake!'

350.

Pierre, a brave French fighter pilot, takes his girlfriend, Marie, out for a pleasant little picnic by the River Seine. It's a beautiful day and love is in the air.

Marie leans over to Pierre and says: 'Pierre, kiss me!' Our hero grabs a bottle of Merlot and splashes it on Marie's lips.

'What are you doing, Pierre?' says the startled Marie.

'I am Pierre the fighter pilot! When I have red meat, I like to have red wine!'

She smiles and they start kissing. When things began to heat up a little, Marie says, 'Pierre, kiss me lower.'

Our hero tears her blouse open, grabs a bottle of Chardonnay and starts pouring it all over her breasts.

'Pierre! What are you doing?' asks the bewildered Marie.

'I am Pierre the fighter pilot! When I have white meat, I like to have white wine!'

They resume their passionate interlude and things really steam up. Marie leans close to his ear and whispers, 'Pierre, kiss me lower!'

Our hero rips off her underwear, grabs a bottle of Cognac and pours it in her lap. He then strikes a match and lights it on fire.

Marie shrieks and dives into the river. Standing waist deep, Marie throws her arms upwards and screams furiously 'Pierre, what in the hell do you think you're doing?!!'

'I am Pierre the fighter pilot! When I go down, I go down in flames!'

351.

After dozens of very expensive tests and weeks of hospitalisation, the rich old man was told he had only 24 hours to live.

He immediately called his doctor and his lawyer to his room. He asked the doctor to stand by one side of his bed and his lawyer to stand by the other.

After standing for some time, the doctor asked 'What do you want me to do?'

'Nothing. Just stand there.'

A while later, the lawyer asked 'What do you want me to do?'

'Nothing. Just stand there.'

As the hours wore on, the doctor and the lawyer watched the man weaken. When his time had almost arrived, the doctor and the lawyer again asked, 'Why are we standing here?'

'Well,' said the old man, 'Christ died between two thieves, so I thought I'd do the same!

352.

A blonde walks into the library. She walks up to the counter, slams a book down and screams at the librarian, 'This is the worst book I've ever read! It has no plot and far too many characters!'

The librarian looks up and calmly remarks – 'Oh, so you're the one who took our phone book . . . '

353.

cats rules

* An aquarium is just interactive television for cats.

* Anything on the ground is a cat toy. Anything not there yet, will be.

* At least dogs do what you tell them to do. Cats take a message and get back to you.

* Buy a dog a toy and it will play with it forever. Buy a cat a present and it will play with the wrapper for ten minutes.

* Cat's motto: No matter what you've done wrong, always try to make it look like the dog did it.

* Cat rule #1: Bite the hand that won't feed you fast enough.

* Cats are rather delicate creatures and they are subject to a good many ailments, but I never heard of one who suffered from insomnia.

* Cats are smarter than dogs. You can't get eight cats to pull a sled through snow.

* Cats aren't clean; they're just covered with cat spit.

* Cats don't hunt seals. They would if they knew what they were and where to find them. But they don't, so that's all right.

* Cats instinctively know the exact moment their owners will wake up. Then they wake them ten minutes sooner.

* Cats know what we feel. They don't care, but they know.

* Cats seem to work on the principle that it never does any harm to ask for what you want.

* Dogs have owners. Cats have staff.

* Dogs believe they are human. Cats believe they are God.

* I had to get rid of my wife. The cat was allergic!

354.

Bernie was invited to his friend's home for dinner. Morris, the host, preceded every request to his wife by endearing terms, calling her Honey, My Love, Darling, Sweetheart, Pumpkin, etc.

Bernie looked at Morris and remarked, 'It's really nice, that after all these years that you have been married you keep calling your wife those pet names.'

Morris hung his head and whispered, 'To tell the truth, I forgot her name three years ago!'

THinGs you'll never hear a woman say

1. What do you mean today's our anniversary?

2. Can we not talk to each other tonight? I'd rather just watch TV.

3. Oh, this diamond ring is way too big!!

4. And for our honeymoon we're going fishing in Alaska!

5. Ah, don't stop for directions, I'm sure you'll be able to figure out how to get there.

6. Is that phone for me? Tell 'em I'm not here.

7. I don't care if it is on sale; $300 is still too much for a designer dress.

KOCHie's Best JOKes 2

356. ways to terrorise a telemarketer

1. Tell them to talk very slowly, because you want to write every word down.

2. Insist that the caller is really your buddy Leon, playing a joke. 'Come on Leon, cut it out! Seriously, Leon, how's your mum?'

3. Tell the telemarketer you are busy at the moment and ask them if they will give you their HOME phone number so you can call them back. When the telemarketer explains that they cannot give out their HOME number, you say 'I guess you don't want anyone bothering you at

home, right?' The telemarketer will agree and you say, 'Now you know how I feel!'

4. After the telemarketer gives their spiel, ask him/her to marry you. When they get all flustered, tell them that you could not just give your credit card number to a complete stranger.

5. Tell the telemarketer you are on 'home incarceration' and ask if they could bring you a case of beer and some chips.

6. If they want to lend you money, tell them you just filed for bankruptcy and you could sure use some money.

7. Cry out in surprise, 'Judy! Is that you? Oh my God! Judy, how have you been?' Hopefully, this will give Judy a few brief moments of pause as she tries to figure out where the hell she could know you from.

8. If they say they're John Doe from XYZ Company, ask them to spell their name. Then ask them to spell the company name. Then ask them where it is located. Continue asking them personal questions or questions about their company for as long as necessary.

9. When they ask 'How are you today?' Tell them! 'I'm so glad you asked because no one these days seems to care, and I have all these problems; my arthritis is acting up, my eyelashes are sore, my dog just died . . . '

2 DAYS BEFORE CHRISTMAS

A mafioso's son sits at his desk writing a Christmas list to Jesus. He first writes, 'Dear baby Jesus, I have been a good boy the whole year, so I want a new . . .' He looks at it, then crumples it up into a ball and throws it away.

He gets out a new piece of paper and writes again, 'Dear baby Jesus, I have been a good boy for most of the year, so I want a new . . .' He again looks at it with disgust and throws it away.

He then gets an idea. He goes into his mother's room, takes a statue of the Virgin Mary, puts it in the closet, and locks the door. He takes another piece of paper and writes, 'Dear baby Jesus. If you ever want to see your mother again . . .'

358.

Sherlock Holmes and Dr. Watson go on a camping trip, set up their tent, and fall asleep. Some hours later, Holmes wakes his faithful friend.

'Watson, look up at the sky and tell me what you see.'

Watson replies, 'I see millions of stars.'

'What does that tell you?'

Watson ponders for a minute. 'Astronomically speaking, it tells me that there are millions of galaxies and potentially billions of planets. Astrologically, it tells me that Saturn is in Leo. Time wise, it appears to be approximately a quarter past three. Theologically, it's evident the Lord is all-powerful and we are small and insignificant. Meteorologically, it seems we will have a beautiful day tomorrow. What does it tell you?'

Holmes is silent for a moment, and then speaks. 'Watson, you idiot, someone has stolen our tent.'

359.

CHRISTMAS DAY

The four stages of life

1. You believe in Santa Claus.

2. You don't believe in Santa Claus.

3. You are Santa Claus.

4. You look like Santa Claus.

360.

Why'd the skeleton cross the road?

To go to the body shop.

361.

* Always take the time to smell the roses . . . and sooner or later you'll inhale a bee.

* If a motorist cuts you off, just turn the other cheek . . . nothing gets the message across like a good mooning.

* If genius is 1% inspiration and 99% perspiration, I must be sharing elevators with a lot of bright people.

* It's always darkest just before dawn . . . so if you're going to steal the neighbours' newspaper, that's the time to do it.

* It takes fewer muscles to smile than to frown . . . and fewer still to ignore someone completely.

* Eagles may soar, but weasels don't get sucked up into jet engines.

* I believe no problem is so large or so difficult that it can't be blamed on someone else.

* If at first you don't succeed, skydiving is not for you.

* It takes a big man to cry . . . But it takes a bigger man to laugh at that man.

* When I'm feeling down I like to whistle . . . it makes my neighbour's dog run to the end of his chain and gag himself.

362.

A woman offered a brand-new car for sale for a price of ten dollars.

A man answered the ad, but he was slightly disbelieving. 'What's the gimmick?' he inquired.

'No gimmick,' the woman answered. 'My husband died, and in his will he asked that the car be sold and the money go to his secretary.'

363.

There are three hunters in the woods. They're all telling each other what they're going to shoot.

The first one says he's going to get a buck. So he goes out and comes back with a buck.

Then the other two hunters ask how he did it and he says, 'I see tracks, I follow tracks, I get buck.'

So the second hunter says, 'I'm going to get a doe.' So he goes out and comes back with a doe.

Then the third hunter asks him how he did it. The second hunter says, 'I see tracks, I follow tracks, I get doe.'

So the third hunter says, 'I'm just going to shoot at anything I see.' So he goes out and comes back half a day later all beaten, bruised bloody and totally trashed.

And the other two hunters ask what happened and he says, 'I see tracks, I follow tracks, I get hit by train!'

364.

A teacher asks her class of third graders to use the word 'fascinate' in a sentence. She calls on a small boy sitting in the front row.

'I saw an air show. And it was very fascinating.'

'Good, but I wanted you to use the word 'fascinate,' not 'fascinating.'' She then calls on a girl sitting off to the left.

'I saw some monkeys. They were very fascinating.'

'Good, but I wanted you to use the world 'fascinate,' not 'fascinating.''

Billy's hand shoots up into the air and she calls on him.

'Teacher, teacher! I got one!'

'Go ahead, Billy.'

'My sister's shirt has ten buttons, but her tits are so big she can only fascinate.'

365.

A blonde woman was having financial troubles so she decided to kidnap a child and demand a ransom.

She went to a local park, grabbed a little boy, took him behind a tree and wrote a note. 'I have kidnapped your child. I am sorry to do this but I need the money. Leave $10,000 in a plain brown bag behind the big oak tree in the park at 7am.' Signed, 'The Blonde.'

She pinned the note inside the little boy's jacket and told him to go straight home.

The next morning, she returned to the park to find the $10,000 in a brown bag behind the big oak tree, just as she had instructed. Inside the bag with the cash was the following note.

'Here is your money. I cannot believe that one blonde would do this to another.'

366.

Three nuns die, but they all have to answer one question to get into Heaven.

The first nun is asked who the first man on earth was. She replies, 'Oh that's easy, Adam!' Lights flash and the Pearly Gates open.

The second nun is asked, 'Who was the first woman on earth?' she says, 'That's easy! Eve!' Lights flash and the gates open.

The third nun is asked, 'What was the first thing Eve said to Adam?

The nun is puzzled and can't figure it out, so she says, 'That's a hard one.'

Lights flash up and the Pearly Gates open.

367.

A priest offered a nun a lift. She got in and crossed her legs, forcing her gown to reveal a leg. The priest nearly had an accident. After controlling the car, he stealthily slid his hand up her leg.

The nun said; 'Father, remember Psalm 129?'

The priest removed his hand. But, changing gears, he let his hand slide up her leg again.

The nun once again said; 'Father, remember Psalm 129?'

The priest apologised; 'Sorry sister but the flesh is weak.'

Arriving at the convent, the nun went on her way.

On his arrival at the church, the priest rushed to look up Psalm 129.

It said; 'Go forth and seek, further up, you will find glory.'

The moral of the story is: If you are not well informed in your job, you might miss a great opportunity.

 368.

What not to say to a cop

* ★ I can't reach my licence unless you hold my beer.

* ★ Sorry, I didn't realise that my radar detector wasn't on.

* ★ Aren't you the guy from the Village People?

* ★ Hey, you must have been going 160k just to keep up with me.

* ★ I thought you had to be in good physical condition to be a cop.

* ★ Bad cop! No donut!

* ★ You're going to check the trunk, aren't you?

* ★ I was going to be a cop, really, but I decided to finish high school.

* ★ I pay your salary.

* ★ That's terrific, the last guy only gave me a warning also.

* ★ Is that a 9mm? It's nothing compared to this .44 Magnum!

* What do you mean, have I been drinking? And you're a trained specialist!

* Do you know why you pulled me over? Good, at least one of us does.

* By the looks of that gut, I bet I can outrun you.

* Is it true people become cops because they are too dumb to work at McDonalds?

* I was trying to keep up with traffic.

* Yes, I know there are no other cars around – that's how far they are ahead of me.

* Well, when I reached down to pick up my bag of crack, my gun fell off my lap and got lodged between the brake pedal and gas pedal, forcing me to speed out of control.

369.

Q. Are you married?

A. No, I'm divorced.

Q. And what did your husband do before you divorced him?

A. A lot of things I didn't know about.

370.

By the time a Marine pulled into a small town, every hotel room was taken.

'You've got to have a room somewhere,' he pleaded. 'Or just a bed, I don't care where.'

'Well, I do have a double room with one occupant; a Navy guy,' admitted the manager, 'and he might be glad to split the cost.

But to tell you the truth, he snores so loudly that people in adjoining rooms have complained in the past, so I'm not sure it'd be worth it to you.'

'No problem,' the tired Marine assured him. 'I'll take it.'

The next morning the Marine came down to breakfast, bright-eyed and bushy-tailed.

'How'd you sleep?' asked the manager.

'Never better.'

The manager was impressed. 'No problem with the other guy snoring, then?'

'Nope, I shut him up in no time,' said the Marine.

'How'd you manage that?' asked the manager.

'He was already in bed, snoring away, when I came in the room,' the Marine explained. 'I went over, gave him a kiss on the cheek, said, Goodnight, beautiful, and he sat up all night watching me.'

371.

A boy from France comes to Australia. He wants to learn some new words so he goes to the airport and learns 'take off.'

Then he learns 'zebra' from the zoo and 'baby' from the hospital. Then he goes home and says, 'Mum, I learned new words today.'

She says, 'Great, honey what did you learn?'

'Takeoffzebrababy!'

372.
Why do women like making love to Greg Norman?

Because he always finishes second!

373.
Bush and Cheney are at a restaurant for lunch. The waitress comes over and asks what they will be having.

Bush says, 'I'll have a quickie.'

The waitress steps back in disgust and says, 'Mr President, I thought that kind of piggish behaviour went out with the last administration!'

She storms off and Dubya looks confused. Cheney shakes his head at the president and says, 'George, it's pronounced QUICHE.'

374.
The government is considering additional warnings on beer and alcohol bottles, such as:

WARNING: Consumption of alcohol may make you think you are whispering when you are not.

WARNING: Consumption of alcohol is a major factor in dancing like an asshole.

WARNING: Consumption of alcohol may cause you to tell the same boring story over and over again until your friends want to SMASH YOUR HEAD IN.

WARNING: Consumption of alcohol may cause you to thay shings like thish.

WARNING: Consumption of alcohol may lead you to believe that ex-lovers are really dying for you to telephone them at four in the morning.

WARNING: Consumption of alcohol may leave you wondering what the hell happened to your pants.

WARNING: Consumption of alcohol may cause you to roll over in the morning and see something really scary (whose species and/or name you can't remember).

WARNING: Consumption of alcohol is the leading cause of inexplicable rug burns on the forehead.

WARNING: Consumption of alcohol may create the illusion that you are tougher, handsomer and smarter than some really, really big guy named Thor.

WARNING: Consumption of alcohol may lead you to believe you are invisible.

WARNING: Consumption of alcohol may lead you to think people are laughing WITH you.

WARNING: Consumption of alcohol may cause a disruption in the space-time continuum, whereby small (and sometimes large) gaps of time may seem to 'disappear'.

WARNING: Consumption of alcohol may actually CAUSE pregnancy.

375.

Q: What should you do if you see your ex-husband rolling around in pain on the ground?

A: Shoot him gain.

376.

Q: What does it mean when a man is in your bed gasping for breath and calling your name?

A: You didn't hold the pillow down long enough.

377.

I went to buy some camouflage trousers the other day but I couldn't find any.